Sir Montague Fowler

Some notable Archbishops of Canterbury

Sir Montague Fowler

Some notable Archbishops of Canterbury

ISBN/EAN: 9783743337619

Manufactured in Europe, USA, Canada, Australia, Japa

Cover: Foto ©ninafisch / pixelio.de

Manufactured and distributed by brebook publishing software (www.brebook.com)

Sir Montague Fowler

Some notable Archbishops of Canterbury

ARCHBISHOP WARHAM.
By permission of His Grace the Archbishop of Canterbury.
FROM THE ORIGINAL PICTURE BY HOLBEIN IN LAMBETH PALACE.

SOME NOTABLE ARCHBISHOPS OF CANTERBURY.

BY THE
REV. MONTAGUE FOWLER, M.A.,
CHAPLAIN TO EDWARD, ARCHBISHOP OF CANTERBURY.

PUBLISHED UNDER THE DIRECTION OF THE TRACT COMMITTEE.

LONDON:
SOCIETY FOR PROMOTING CHRISTIAN KNOWLEDGE,
NORTHUMBERLAND AVENUE, W.C.;
43, QUEEN VICTORIA STREET, E.C.
BRIGHTON: 129, NORTH STREET.
NEW YORK: E. & J. B. YOUNG AND CO.
1895.

DEDICATED

TO

EDWARD,

NINETY-SECOND ARCHBISHOP OF CANTERBURY,

WITH AFFECTIONATE APPRECIATION

OF

MANY KINDNESSES RECEIVED

DURING

SIX YEARS' RESIDENCE AND WORK

AT

LAMBETH PALACE,

BY

THE AUTHOR.

PREFATORY REMARKS.

THE writer claims neither originality of thought nor depth of research in regard to the following memoirs. But he believes that the attempt to give, in brief outline, the main facts in the lives of some of the greatest occupants of the chair of St. Augustine may assist in bringing home to many readers the grand historic continuity of the Anglican branch of the Catholic Church.

He gratefully acknowledges his indebtedness to Dean Hook's valuable work in compiling the accounts of the earlier archbishops, and to the Bishop of Rochester's most attractive life of Archbishop Tait. His best thanks are due to Canon Erskine Clarke for permission to use the excellent reproductions of the Lambeth portraits.

M. F.

APRIL, 1895.

CONTENTS.

CHAPTER		PAGE
I.	AUGUSTINE (597–604) ...	7
II.	THEODORE (669–690) ...	20
III.	ANSELM (1093–1109). *Portrait of Grindal* ...	34
IV.	BECKET (1162–1171) ...	48
V.	CHICHELEY (1414–1443) ...	62
VI.	WARHAM (1503–1532). *With Portrait* ...	76
VII.	CRANMER (1533–1556). *With Portrait* ...	89
VIII.	PARKER (1559–1575). *With Portrait* ...	101
IX.	LAUD (1633–1645). *With Portrait* ...	113
X.	SANCROFT (1678–1693) ...	126
XI.	HOWLEY (1828–1848). *Portrait of Whitgift* ...	139
XII.	SUMNER (1848–1862) ...	154
XIII.	LONGLEY (1862–1868) ...	170
XIV.	TAIT (1869–1882) ...	186
APPENDIX A.	SUCCESSION OF THE ARCHBISHOPS OF CANTERBURY ...	203
,, B.	BRIEF MEMOIRS OF THE ARCHBISHOPS OF CANTERBURY ...	205
,, C.	CONSECRATIONS BY THE ARCHBISHOPS ...	210
INDEX	...	219

NOTABLE ARCHBISHOPS OF CANTERBURY.

CHAPTER I.

AUGUSTINE (597–604 A.D.).

JUST as the civil history of England is closely bound up in the lives of the monarchs who have occupied the throne of this land, so the religious history of the nation centres round the person and character of those men who have been called, by Divine Providence, to preside over the destinies of the National Church.

The exact date of the introduction of Christianity into Britain is uncertain, and we have no evidence to show by whom the gospel was originally preached to the Celts, the first known inhabitants of these islands. Tertullian ("Adv. Judæos," c. 7) states that the regions of Britain, inaccessible to the Romans, were subdued to Christ in the second century; and other authorities assert that this was effected by missionaries from the East, either by direct communication, or through the Churches of Gaul.

The history of the British Church, like its origin,

is involved in obscurity. The Anglo-Saxons, after their conquest, appear to have destroyed the documents which came into their possession, or else to have allowed them to perish. We have, however, sufficient evidence to show that among the Irish (or Scots), the Caledonians, the Welsh, and the British, during the fourth and fifth centuries, the learning, zeal, and piety of the Church had extended widely, and had obtained a firm hold over the religious aspirations of the people.

We know that British bishops attended the Council of Arles in 314 A.D., of Sardica in 347 A.D., and of Ariminum in 360 A.D. We know that with such leaders as St. Patrick among the Irish, St. Ninian in the North, and St. Columba in Scotland, the spiritual life of the inhabitants of these islands could not have been altogether at a low ebb. At the same time, the troubled political conditions that prevailed, and the successive invasions of the Picts, the Jutes, and the Saxons (rendering an established and settled form of government hopeless and impracticable), militated severely against such religious growth as might otherwise have been anticipated.

Gradually the seven Anglo-Saxon kingdoms were formed under the name of the Heptarchy; but, unfortunately, the civil improvement of the country was disastrous to the ancient British Church. During the 150 years' struggle, the Britons were driven further and further westward; prelates, priests, and people were destroyed together by fire and sword; and the Christian sanctuaries were demolished.

Towards the close of the sixth century we find

that the great city of Rome had declined in power owing to the transfer of the seat of government to Constantinople, and the Bishop of Rome, being the only important person remaining in residence, became its virtual ruler. The story of Gregory, then archdeacon, and the English slaves, is told by Bede ("Eccl. Hist.," bk. ii. c. 1). The pagan condition of the "Angles," as explained to him at that time, remained in his memory, and when, a few years later, he succeeded to the papal chair, he sent over some monks under Augustine to preach the gospel of Christ.

While it is perfectly true that the majority of the Anglo-Saxon inhabitants of our country were heathens at the time when Augustine landed on our shores, yet it must be remembered that many circumstances combined to render them peculiarly receptive of Christian teaching. There was the germ, in their own superstitions, of a belief in a Supreme Being, which would be certain to spring forth when the cult of Woden, the god of slaughter, gave place to the teaching of Jesus Christ. Again, the feeling of contempt for the religion of the race they had conquered and persecuted (which led them to turn a deaf ear to the preaching of the British bishops and priests) was considerably modified by the fact that this same Christianity was held by the Goths in Italy, Spain, and Southern France; by the Lombards and the Franks; and by the Romans, who were objects of admiration and respect among all the barbarian races. Once more, the fact that many of the pagan Saxons, who came over as warriors, had married British wives, renders it certain that a powerful religious influence in the direction of Christian truth must have been quietly working its way, and preparing the soil for the germination of the seed to be sown by the foreign missionaries.

Of the early life of Augustine nothing is known. He appears to have succeeded Gregory (who became Bishop of Rome in 590 A.D.) as Prior of the Benedictine Monastery of St. Andrew, in that city; and to have been at the time somewhat advanced in years.

Accompanied by forty monks (regular and secular), Augustine set forth in 596 A.D. to undertake the task of converting the inhabitants of the British Isles. The party rapidly traversed the northern portion of Italy, crossed the Gallic Alps, and arrived in Provence. Here they began to lose heart and courage. They were surprised to find an unkindly spirit manifested by the French, and the authority of the Bishop of Rome set at naught. Realizing that their difficulties had commenced, and that opposition had arisen, before they had even reached their destination, the whole party became so disheartened and alarmed that Augustine returned to Gregory, seeking permission to abandon the enterprise.

We find in this incident the first indication of the fact, which is strikingly brought out in his subsequent career, that Augustine was by no means a master-mind. Had he been a man of more powerful character, he would have been able to dispel the fears of his companions, and to encourage them by pointing out the magnitude of the work that lay before them, and the necessity of overcoming, instead of being overcome by, the trials that must of necessity await them in the accomplishment of the task they had undertaken.

Gregory, who had manfully risen above difficulties far greater than those encountered by the missionaries, despatched Augustine to his timid companions, bearing a letter in which the following sentences occur: "Forasmuch as it were better not to begin a good work than to think of desisting from that which has been begun, it behoves you, my beloved sons, to accomplish the good work on which, by the help of the Lord, you have entered. Let not, therefore, the toil of the journey, nor the tongues of evil-speaking men, deter you; but with all possible earnestness and zeal, perform that which, by God's direction, you have undertaken; being assured that much labour is followed by greater eternal reward. When Augustine, your leader, returns, humbly obey him in all things. . . ." (Bede, "Eccl. Hist.," bk. i. c. 23).

At length, after many vicissitudes, the missionary band arrived in England early in 597 A.D. They landed in the Isle of Thanet, probably at Ebbsfleet, where they remained in a state of considerable trepidation until the interpreters whom they had sent to King Ethelbert returned. The message they received, however, dispelled all their fears, and preparations were made for an interview.

Ethelbert, King of Kent (one of the seven divisions of the Heptarchy), was a noble-hearted, liberal-minded, intelligent man. He had married Bertha, daughter of Charibert, King of Paris, who was herself an earnest Christian. It had been stipulated, as a condition of her marriage, that she should enjoy the free exercise of her religion, and she came to England attended by her chaplain, Luidhard, formerly Bishop of Senlis, a man of considerable age. His influence at the court was by no means slight, and helped, together with the gentle piety of his royal mistress, to induce the household to view with favour the religion of their queen. He received from Ethelbert an old Roman (or British) church in which to hold services, consecrated it afresh, and named it after St. Martin. The church (or at least a portion of it) is still standing, a silent witness to the power of Christ's teaching for sixteen centuries in the land.

In due course it was announced to Augustine that the king would receive the missionaries, but that the meeting must take place in the open air. He did not conceal his fear that otherwise recourse might be had to magical arts, and his judgment be unduly biassed.

A procession was accordingly formed, at the head of which walked Augustine, who is described as a tall, powerfully built, swarthy-complexioned man, preceded by a crucifer bearing a silver cross (the crucifix did not at that time exist, its first appearance dating from the close of the seventh century); then came an oil-painting representing the figure of our Blessed Lord, behind which followed the brethren in order. Slowly and solemnly marched the little band along the shores of Pegwell Bay, chanting in unison one of those solemn litanies introduced from the Eastern Church, which must have riveted the attention, and impressed the minds, of those who were waiting with anxious and curious expectancy for the arrival of these strangers. The king, accompanied by the queen, and surrounded by his soldiers and wise men, was seated under an ancient oak. The site of what is believed to have been the identical tree is marked by a granite cross, close to the village of Cliffsend.

Ethelbert received the missionaries with courteous dignity, and listened with attention to the sermon which Augustine preached, by means of interpreters, wherein he told "how the merciful Jesus, by His own Passion, redeemed this guilty world, and opened to believing men an entrance into the kingdom of heaven." The king's reply is interesting. "Very fair," he said, "are the words you have uttered and the promises you make. But to us these things are new, and their full meaning I do not understand. I am by no means prepared to assent to proposals which imply the renunciation of customs to which, with the whole English race, I have hitherto adhered. But you have come from far. You are strangers. And I clearly perceive that your sole wish and only object is to communicate to us what you believe to be good and true. You shall not be molested. You shall be hospitably entertained. We will make provision for your maintenance, and we do not prohibit you from uniting to your society any persons whom you may persuade to embrace your faith" (Bede, "Eccl. Hist.," bk. i. c. 25).

Augustine and his companions settled in Canterbury. They lived in primitive simplicity, "applying themselves to frequent prayer, watching, and fasting; preaching the Word of life to as many as would hear them; receiving only their necessary food from those they taught; living in all respects conformably to what they prescribed for others, and being always disposed to suffer any adversity, and even to die, for the truth which they preached. In short, several believed and were baptized, admiring the simplicity of their innocent life, and the sweetness of their heavenly doctrine."

At length, on the 2nd of June, 597 A.D., being the feast of Whitsunday, Ethelbert openly declared himself a Christian, and received the Sacrament of Baptism. About the same time the Witan assembled, at which the counsellors and wise men concurred with the king in enacting what are called the "Dooms of Ethelbert." These laws recognized Christianity and the Christian priesthood, and established the Church in the kingdom of Kent. This official acknowledgment of the faith on the part of the king and his counsellors had such an effect upon the people that on the following Christmas Day ten thousand persons were baptized.

Such an accession of numbers required an increase both of Church accommodation and of clergy. The former was provided by the liberality of the king, who not only gave up his palace at Canterbury as a residence for Augustine, but also, on the site of an ancient church close by, laid the foundation of the cathedral, which has ever since borne the name of Christ's Church. He endowed a monastery, originally called after St. Peter and St. Paul; but its name was subsequently changed, and as the Missionary College of St. Augustine, it still stands as a blessing to the Church of which Augustine was the first archbishop.

For additional clergy application was made to Gregory, who sent a further band of missionaries with valuable gifts, consisting of altar-cloths, vestments, and books. Among the new arrivals were Mellitus, afterwards Bishop of London; Justus, Bishop of Rochester (both of whom succeeded to the primacy); and Paulinus, afterwards Archbishop of York.

In 597 A.D. Augustine repaired to France in accordance with instructions from Gregory, and was consecrated by Vergilius, Archishop of Arles, to be "Bishop of the English," that he might be at liberty to fix his see either in London or Canterbury, or in whatever part of the country he deemed advisable. Immediately on his return he set about the organization of a complete ecclesiastical scheme for the whole country. Twelve bishoprics were to be founded in the south of England. Twelve more were to form a northern province. There was to be a metropolitan see at York, but it was to be subject to Augustine's supremacy. He did not, however, live to carry out the plan, although it served as a basis for the future framework of the Church.

A difficult question of administration soon presented itself to Augustine for solution, and he immediately sought counsel from Gregory. Being perplexed at the differences in the customs ruling in various Churches, he was enjoined, in preparing a liturgy for the Anglican Church, not to tie himself down to the Roman ritual, or of the Gallican, or to any other, but to select out of every Church what is pious, religious, and right; for "things are not to be valued on account of places, but places for the good things they contain."

Another point which was submitted for advice was this: "How are we to deal with the bishops of France and Britain?" Writing doubtless in ignorance of the deep-rooted animosity which divided Briton and Saxon, Gregory ordered that the new archiepiscopate in Ethelbert's dominions should control not only all bishops consecrated by Augustine, or by the future Archbishop of York, but also all the priests of Britain. "Over the bishops of France," the letter runs, "we give you no authority, because the Bishop of Arles received the pall in ancient times from my predecessor, and we ought by no means to deprive him of the authority he has received; . . . but as for all the bishops of Britain, we commit them to your care, that the unlearned may be taught, the feeble strengthened by persuasion, and the perverse corrected by authority" (Bede, "Eccl. Hist.," bk. i. c. 27).

Having received from Gregory the coveted distinction of the pallium, and being fortified by the instructions given him in the letter referred to, Augustine determined at once to call upon the British bishops to acknowledge him in the character of Metropolitan, and to submit to his supremacy.

It must be remembered that for three hundred and fifty years or more the Church in Britain had kept the faith unaided by popes or papal delegates. It knew nothing of Rome, but it had cause to know and distrust the Saxon princes who were Rome's present allies. No slight measure of gentleness, forbearance, and tact was needed if Augustine was to be successful in uniting and consolidating, under the Archbishop of Canterbury, the two branches (one recently implanted from abroad, the other the ancient religion of the nation) of the Holy Catholic Church.

Unfortunately, as we shall see, neither the education nor the temper of Augustine fitted him for so difficult and delicate a position. A meeting was arranged at a place called Augustine's Oak (probably at Austcliffe on the Severn). The new archbishop commenced by calling upon the representatives of the Celtic Church to unite with him in the conversion of the heathen, a duty which was of course admitted by all. And then, assuming without proof that he was right and they were wrong, he demanded, as the condition of such fellowship, the surrender of certain principles, and the renunciation of certain practices, which were the peculiarities of the Celtic Churches, and were, as marks of their independence, especially dear to them.

For example, the question arose as to the day on which Easter should be kept. The British bishops adhered to the old Western rule laid down at the Council of Nicæa in 325 A.D., by which they kept the festival of the Resurrection on the 14th day of the Paschal moon, whether it fell on a Sunday or not. Augustine, on the other hand, declared in favour of the practice, which had, not long before, been adopted by the Roman Church (in order to effect a uniformity with the Church of Alexandria), of observing the Sunday following the 14th day of the Paschal moon (if the 14th fell on a Sunday) as the Easter festival. He demanded that the British bishops should at once alter their usage, but they were inflexible. Augustine remonstrated, exhorted, grew angry, and sternly rebuked them. He then attempted to win them over by the cure of a blind man whom they had previously attempted, in vain, to heal.

A second conference was arranged for a later date. Meanwhile a preliminary meeting of the British bishops was held. On the advice of a holy and learned anchorite, it was decided that if Augustine showed himself to be possessed of the spirit of Christian humility by rising to receive them, they were to agree to his proposals, and accept him as their leader. They came, and Augustine received them seated. Thereupon they refused to concede any one point of the three laid down, viz. the observance of Easter according to the Roman computation, the adoption of the Roman form of triple immersion in Baptism, and the uniting with him in evangelizing the Saxons. At this Augustine lost his temper, and parted from them, predicting that "they who refused to show their neighbours the way of life should by them be put to death."

Augustine now returned to Canterbury, where he was enabled to pursue, for the short remainder of his life, the even tenor of his way, in a sphere more suited to his temper, his capacities, and his many virtues.

In considering his arrogance towards the representatives of the British Church, we must bear in mind that he failed to appreciate their position and learning. He regarded them as semi-barbarians, and despised them on account of their subjection to the pagan Saxons. He was, moreover, led away by the unwarrantable assumption of authority over the British Church which Gregory claimed, an assumption totally opposed to the decrees of the

Council of Ephesus, which stipulated that "no bishop shall occupy another province that has not been subject to him from the beginning."

Augustine, with all his faults—among which may be included his somewhat high-handed and irregular proceeding in nominating, appointing, and consecrating his successor during his own lifetime, in contravention of the decrees of the Councils of Nicæa and Antioch—was greatly revered and beloved by his contemporaries. He died in 604 A.D., and was buried near the unfinished Church of St. Peter and St. Paul, in the ground now occupied by the Kent and Canterbury Hospital.

Augustine's visit to England was really but one episode in a record of missionary enterprise extending over a period of upwards of a century. The actual area of his success was limited. Under his leadership Kent and Essex became for a time Christian settlements, and a work in Northumberland, commenced by his companion Paulinus, flourished for a short period, until it was swept away when the reigning dynasty was ousted by the heathen Penda. At the same time, a peculiar interest attaches to this Roman mission in that it laid the foundation of our existing ecclesiastical organization. Other missionaries, natives of these islands, shared in the glory of winning converts to Christianity; but Gregory and Augustine inaugurated the system by which, when resuscitated by Theodore, those converts became the body of the Anglican Church, which has held its position in unbroken succession to the present day, and still flourishes, as essentially the Church of the nation.

CHAPTER II.

THEODORE (669-690 A.D.).

AUGUSTINE was succeeded in the primacy by Laurentius, who had accompanied him on his mission to King Ethelbert in 597 A.D. Within a few years the kingdoms of Kent and Essex relapsed into paganism, but by influences which Bede connects with supernatural occurrences, although to us they seem to have been of the nature of "pious frauds," the new king, Eadbald, was prevailed upon to embrace the Christian faith, and his example was soon followed by his subjects. Paulinus, who became the first Archbishop of York, had a temporary success in the north; but shortly after the death of Edwin a pagan reaction set in, and within sixty years of the landing of Augustine the visible results of the labours of the Roman missionaries had to a great extent disappeared.

Meanwhile the work of Christianizing the north was steadily proceeding under St. Aidan and other British preachers. In course of time the two missionary systems came into collision. The British bishops still adhered to the customs and practices which had excited the anger of Augustine; but the question at issue was finally settled at the Synod of Streanæshalc (Whitby), in 664 A.D., when the pretensions of the papacy won the victory for the foreign ritual, and the acceptance of the Roman method of observing Easter prepared England for a definite system of Church order and uniformity such as Gregory had contemplated.

The next event of importance in the religious history of this country was the consolidation of the independent Heptarchic sees into a National Church. We shall deal with this at some length in the present chapter.

Frithona, the first Saxon Archbishop of Canterbury, who is better known by his adopted Latin appellation Deusdedit, died in 664 A.D. The kings of Northumbria and Kent selected Wighard as his successor, and sent him to Rome for consecration, but he died shortly after his arrival. The see of Canterbury having, from one cause or another, been vacant for nearly four years, the kings agreed to leave the choice of Wighard's successor in the hands of Pope Vitalian. The Bishop of Rome, well aware of the conditions of ecclesiastical life in Northumbria, where Wilfrid and Chad were rival bishops of York, realized that it would be imprudent to send an Italian to the metropolitical see of the south. He knew no Englishman suitable for the post. At length he fixed his choice upon an African, Hadrian by name. Hadrian was a learned monk, and he declined the offer, desiring to continue to devote himself to his books; but he recommended his friend Theodore, a native of Tarsus, who was consecrated at Rome in March, 668 A.D. This is the first instance of the direct consecration of an archbishop for the British Isles by the Roman pontiff, and after Theodore there was not another Roman archbishop for three hundred and fifty years, all who succeeded him being Englishmen. After a year's journey, Theodore, accompanied by Hadrian, and also by Benedict Biscop, whose name is famous both as a builder of churches and as a collector of literary treasures, arrived in England in May, 669 A.D., and on the 27th day of the same month was installed in St. Augustine's chair as seventh Archbishop of Canterbury, amidst great rejoicings. He was then sixty-six years of age, but he entered with all the ardour of youth upon the vigorous discharge of his duties, and the development of that complete system of ecclesiastical organization which has made his memory famous.

Immediately after his enthronement the new primate made a general visitation of his province, inspecting the monasteries, establishing schools, and correcting abuses. He was welcomed everywhere, both by the princes and nobles and by the clergy. He returned to Canterbury when his tour was ended, resolved to accomplish two aims; first, to lay the foundation of what we now call the parochial system, and secondly, to increase the episcopate.

At that date the Church of England, whether we turn to the Celtic Churches, or to those which were the outcome of St. Augustine's mission, consisted simply of a number of missionary centres. From these the clergy went forth to preach the gospel in the towns and outlying hamlets, and even to the remote caves of the bandits and outlaws, not unfrequently being absent for weeks at a time. But besides the clergy who were engaged in missionary labours, there were others who were attached to the households of the princes and the thanes, in the capacity of private chaplains. It was on this foundation that Theodore built his plan for the formation of separate parishes, where the priest would be resident among his people, and the preaching of the Word and administration of the sacraments could be carried on without interruption. He persuaded the nobles and landed proprietors to assign to their former chaplains an independent position, to erect churches in the centre of their estates, and to provide endowments by grants of land, or fixed charges upon their properties. In order to encourage the landowners to do this systematically, Theodore arranged that those who agreed to carry out the scheme should have the right of selecting their resident parish clergyman ; and we thus trace the origin of our present system of private patronage, and of ecclesiastical districts. It is interesting to notice that the Church, as has been almost universally the case throughout her history, set the example which was subsequently followed by the secular government. Green, in his "History of the English People," says, "The regular subordination of priest to bishop and of bishop to primate, in the administration of the Church, supplied a mould on which the civil organization of the State quickly shaped itself." And "it was the ecclesiastical synods which by their example led the way to our National Parliament, as it was the canons enacted in such synods which led the way to a national system of law."

In carrying out his scheme for the extension of the episcopate, Theodore was equally vigorous, and, notwithstanding considerable opposition, was equally successful. Within a few years he constituted seventeen bishoprics where there had formerly been only nine. Kent, Essex, and Sussex were considered to be sufficiently provided with episcopal supervision, and were not interfered with. East Anglia had the see of Elmham added to that of Dunwich; Wessex was in future to become two dioceses, Winchester and Sherborne; and the great midland province of Mercia was now divided into five sections, with the bishops' seats at Lichfield, Hereford, Worcester, Leicester, and Lindsey. In Northumbria the primate encountered the greatest opposition, but finally the gigantic diocese of York was made into four dioceses —those of Hexham, Whithern, and Lindisfarne.

When visiting Northumbria soon after his enthronement (for at that time York was not a metropolitan see, and the whole of England was in the province of Canterbury), Theodore exercised his authority by deposing Ceadda, or Chad, and replacing Wilfrid. Wilfrid had been consecrated in France to the see of York in 664 A.D., but by his arrogance at the Council of Whitby, and his prolonged residence abroad, he had alienated the affection and popularity which had been at first extended to him. Chad was a monk belonging to the monastery of Lastingham, and the people of Northumbria petitioned their king, Oswy, that Chad might be their bishop. The king agreed, whereupon Chad, after his consecration at Winchester, proceeded north, and threw himself heart and soul into his episcopal work. When Wilfrid returned to Britain, he found his rival on the spot; but, realizing that he had lost favour with the Northumbrians, he contented himself with administering the diocese of Canterbury between the death of Deusdedit and the arrival of Theodore. On being restored to the temporalities of the see of York, Wilfrid immediately set to work to restore the cathedral, which he found in a dilapidated condition. A reaction set in in his favour to such an extent that vast sums of money were left to him. He immediately adopted an almost royal state, with princely retinues, and the most extravagant expenditure, until he excited the enmity of Ecgfrid the king, on account of his opposition to the marriage with Irminburga, after the king had separated from his first wife, Etheldreda.

Such was the state of affairs in the north when Archbishop Theodore proposed the subdivision of the diocese of Northumbria. Wilfrid could not, on ecclesiastical grounds, oppose the scheme; but, unwilling to diminish his pomp and splendour, or to relinquish his power, he resisted the primate, who thereupon, with the support of the court behind him, uttered a sentence of deposition upon Wilfrid, and consecrated Bosa as his successor, in the year 678 A.D.

The Bishop of York, indignant at this treatment, repaired to Rome, where he appealed against the decision. Naturally the Bishop of Rome, desirous above all things of establishing a claim to exercise jurisdiction and authority in the English Church, decided in Wilfrid's favour. But the country was in no mood to recognise the interference of the papacy in her ecclesiastical affairs. Consequently, when Wilfrid returned, and produced the demand of Pope Agatho that he should be reinstated in his office and privileges, the king convened a council of the nobility and clergy of his kingdom, and it was unanimously determined that the appeal to Rome was a public offence, and that the papal letters were an insult to the crown and nation. Wilfrid was condemned to nine months' imprisonment, and became for many years a wandering outcast.

The pope's mandate, threatening excommunication to all who disobeyed it, was disregarded and treated with utter indifference by Archbishop Theodore. This fact is interesting, because it shows that the principle of Roman dictation in the affairs of the Church of England was firmly resisted in the early days of its attempted enforcement; and when, later on, we find that the Bishop of Rome did exert his authority, it was because, by his alliance with the sovereign, he proved too strong for our Church rulers to resist, although in almost every case the submission was made under protest.

Besides the two great schemes, on the accomplishment of which Theodore had set his heart, viz. the development of the parochial system, and the extension of the episcopate, it was part of his plan to introduce synodical action into the Church. His aim was to hold synods twice in every year, but in this he does not appear to have succeeded. He managed, however, to convene two important councils during his episcopate.

The first was held on September 24, 673 A.D., at Hertford, and was attended by all the leading bishops. Wilfrid, Bishop of York, was represented by two of his clergy.

The archbishop first asked those assembled if they would defer to whatever was decreed canonically and of old by the fathers. On their expressing a unanimous assent, he submitted ten articles from a collection of canons that had been approved by the Council of Chalcedon in A.D. 451, and accepted by the Western Church. These were adapted, after careful discussion, to the needs of the English Church, and all the prelates and clergy present bound themselves by signing their names to the draft, to observe the rules, which were as follows:—

1. That there should be uniformity in keeping Easter on the Sunday after the 14th day of the first month.

2. That no bishop should intrude into another's diocese.

3. That no bishop should disturb the monasteries, or seize their property.

4. That monks should not move from one monastery to another without leave of their own abbot.

5. That the clergy should not go from their diocese without leave, nor be received in another diocese without commendatory letters from their former bishop.

6. That bishops and clergy, when travelling,

should not presume to officiate without the licence of the bishop in whose diocese they may be.

7. That a yearly synod should be held, on August 1, at Clofeshoch (or Cloveshoo).

8. That no bishop, through ambition, should try to take precedence of another; but that each should observe the time and order of his consecration.

9. That, as the number of the faithful increased, bishops should be multiplied.

10. That marriages should not be made within the prohibited degrees; that no divorce, except as the gospel teaches, should be permitted; and that no one who has divorced his wife may marry again.

It was immediately after this council that Theodore set him seriously to work to carry out the subdivision of the dioceses, of which mention has been made above.

Theodore, when he disregarded the anathema of the Bishop of Rome, consequent on his refusing to accede to the papal demand for reinstating Wilfrid, was equally regardless of the pope's wish that he should attend the third Council of Constantinople, in 680 A.D., which had been convened to condemn the Monothelite heresy—*i.e.* the heresy which denied the existence of two wills, the human and the Divine, in our Blessed Lord.

He considered it more important to convene a council in England, in order to ascertain the exact faith held by the Church at home, in reference to the various heresies that had arisen in other parts of the Christian world. The synod was held at Hatfield, on September 17, 680 A.D. The archbishop caused the proceedings to be taken down in writing, and the document is preserved for us in Bede's "Ecclesiastical History," iv. 17. After setting forth what the assembled prelates held as the true faith of the Catholic Church in regard to the doctrine of the Holy Trinity, the following passage occurs: "We have received the five holy and general councils of the blessed fathers acceptable to God; that is, of the three hundred and eighteen bishops who were assembled at Nicæa (325 A.D.), against the most impious Arius and his tenets; and that at Constantinople (381 A.D.) of the one hundred and fifty, against the madness of Macedonius and Eudoxius and their tenets; and that first at Ephesus (431 A.D.) of the two hundred, against the most wicked Nestorius and his tenets; and that at Chalcedon (451 A.D.) of the six hundred and thirty, against Eutyches and Nestorius and their tenets; and again at Constantinople (553 A.D.), in a fifth council, in the reign of Justinian the younger, against Theodorus and the Epistles of Theodoret and Ibas, and their tenets, against Cyril." These five councils are still the authority for the faith of the Church in Britain, as they had been of the Celtic Church long before the coming of Theodore.

In addition to the active and administrative work of Archbishop Theodore, which we have briefly described, his name is almost equally famous as the founder of Anglo-Saxon scholarship and literature. Within a very short time after his enthronement at Canterbury, he took possession of St. Augustine's monastery, and made it a school of learning. In his friend Hadrian Theodore found an able coadjutor. He is described by William of

Malmesbury as "a fountain of letters and a river of arts." These great men understood the importance of encouraging a learned clergy, and they found the English people eager to be instructed. Bede tells us ("Eccl. Hist.," iv. 2) how "both of them, being well read both in sacred and in secular literature, gathered a crowd of disciples, and there daily flowed from them rivers of knowledge to water the hearts of their hearers; and, together with the books of Holy Writ, they also taught them the arts of ecclesiastical poetry, astronomy, and arithmetic." Through their influence all the larger and better monasteries, as well as some of the convents, became seminaries of learning. In the next century English scholars, such as Bede and Alcuin, had won a European reputation, and the skill of our monastic copyists became proverbial. "In a single century England became known as a fountain of light, as a land of learned men, devout and unwearied missions, of strong, rich, and pious kings" (Stubbs, "Const. Hist.," i. 219). Theodore, who had been famous as a Greek divine before he came to England, introduced into this country a class of studies almost unknown in Western Christendom. He obtained from the East a large number of Greek copies of the Gospels, two of which are still extant; one, being Codex E, is in the Bodleian Library at Oxford, and the other is preserved at Corpus Christi College, Cambridge.

Archbishop Theodore held a high position as an author. His "Penitential" is a remarkable book, not so much on the ground that it was the first work of the kind that had ever appeared, which was not the case, but because it was the earliest of the "libelli pœnitentiales" that was published by authority in the Western Church, and was the foundation on which other books of the same nature were based, such as those issued by Bede and by Egbert. His rules and regulations concerning penance, confession, Church discipline, etc., were couched in a far more severe strain than would be approved in those days, but were, perhaps, well suited to the circumstances of histories.

The career of the octogenarian archbishop was now drawing rapidly to a close, and most of the aims which Theodore had set before himself had been accomplished. The metropolitan authority of the see of Canterbury was universally acknowledged; the largest dioceses had been divided; parishes had begun to be arranged, and in some cases parish boundaries had been settled; parochial churches had been everywhere erected; moral discipline was enforced; the foundation had been laid for a thorough system of learning and scholarship, while the state of the country under Theodore's archiepiscopate is thus described by Bede (iv. 2): "Happier times than these never were since the English came into Britain; for their kings were brave men and good Christians, and while, by the terror of their arms, the barbarians were kept in check, the minds of men were bent upon the joys of the heavenly kingdom which had just been revealed to them; and every one who desired instruction in the sacred Scriptures had masters at hand to instruct him."

Before his death, Theodore sought to be reconciled with Wilfrid. Since his deposition from the see of Northumbria, the latter had found employment for his active and zealous mind in the conversion of Sussex, the only kingdom of the Heptarchy which, up to this time, adhered to paganism. When, in a season of scarcity, he taught the natives how to catch fish, he was hailed with joy as their deliverer, and soon established a bishopric at Selsey, where he erected a cathedral, and established a chapter of secular canons. In the reign of William the Conqueror the cathedral was removed to Chichester, which became the head-quarters of the bishops of that county from that time. At length, shortly before the death of Theodore, a meeting with Wilfrid was effected through the instrumentality of Erkenwald, Bishop of London; and, in consequence of the influence of the archbishop with Alfrid, the successor of Ecgfrid in the throne of Northumbria, Wilfrid was reinstated as bishop of the northern diocese.

Theodore died on September 19, 690 A.D., at the age of eighty-seven, and was buried by the side of his predecessors in the porch of St. Augustine's. He was a prelate more powerful in many ways than his predecessor, St. Augustine, and was possessed of a greater amount of tact, and had his temper under better control. There is little doubt that, with the example of the first Archbishop of Canterbury before him, he would have nominated Wilfrid to be his successor, had he considered him a fit person for the post. But the requisites for so responsible a position were energy and sound judgment. The northern prelate had more than enough of the first, but was lamentably deficient in the second. And so the aged primate, whose kindly nature showed itself in many ways, notably when he obtained for Chad (who retired without a murmur in favour of Wilfrid, under circumstances already mentioned) the see of Lichfield, determined to do his utmost to benefit the able, though unwise, bishop, by procuring his reappointment to the Northumbrian see.

To Theodore we owe the change in the character of the English Church, that he raised it from the position of a missionary station into a completely organized and thoroughly consolidated National Church.

CHAPTER III.

ANSELM (1093–1109 A.D.).

THE effect of Theodore's work in bringing about a unification of the English Church under a recognised head, and organized upon a uniform plan, soon made itself felt throughout the country. The clergy became the advisers of the people in temporal as well as spiritual affairs, and no important laws were made without consulting them. The bishops sat side by side with the nobles in the Witan to adjudicate upon the social, political, and domestic needs of the nation; and the unity of the Church frequently enabled her authorities to prevent strife, and even bloodshed, when quarrels arose between the different kingdoms.

The religious enthusiasm which arose at this time found an outlet in the growth of the monastic system, and the increase of pilgrimages. The instances of Anglo-Saxon princes and princesses who exchanged the court for the cloister are too numerous to be detailed. Ceolwulf of Northumbria, about 725 A.D., is said to have been the eighth king who assumed the garb of a monk.

In 747 A.D. an important council was held at Cloveshoo, at which thirty canons were passed. It

ARCHBISHOP GRINDAL.
By permission of His Grace the Archbishop of Canterbury.
FROM THE PORTRAIT BY MARTIN DE VOS IN THE COLLECTION AT
LAMBETH PALACE.

was enacted that the people should learn the Creed and the Lord's Prayer, and be instructed in the nature of the sacraments; prayers for the dead were to be offered; and the bishops were to visit their dioceses annually. A general conformity with the usages of Rome was enjoined, but no submission to papal authority was sanctioned, it being expressly stated that the highest court of appeal in ecclesiastical matters was to the archbishop in synod.

In 787 A.D. this submission to the pope was rendered by Offa, King of Mercia, in furtherance of his own ambition. Being anxious to curtail the dignity and authority of the Archbishop of Canterbury, he established a new archiepiscopal see at Lichfield, which, however, only existed for twenty years. To effect this, and to obtain a pall for the new metropolitan, he gave enormous bribes to the papal see.

The religious prosperity of England was wrecked during the ninth century by the Danish invasion. Bishops and clergy fled from their benefices, and the religious houses were for the most part pillaged and destroyed. After the defeat of the invaders by Alfred at Ethandune, in 878 A.D., the restoration of the Church and her work went on rapidly, and many of the Danes were converted to Christianity.

Throughout the ninth and tenth centuries the claims of Roman supremacy were put forward whenever opportunity offered; but it is significant that in no instance was this state of things recognised or accepted at the many synods of the Anglican Church during that period.

The conquest of England by William of Normandy introduced a new era in the history of the Church. In Anglo-Saxon times the relations of Church and State were for the most part of a friendly nature. One of William's first acts was, with the help of the papal legates sent by Gregory VII., to depose Stigand from the archbishopric of Canterbury, and to replace him by Lanfranc. The powers and privileges of the bishops were curtailed. The papal claims upon the allegiance of the Church were encouraged by the king, although he did not scruple to resist the pope where his own interests were concerned. We see this in William's reply to the demand that he should do homage to Gregory. "Homage to thee," he said, "I have not chosen, neither do I choose to do. I never made a promise to that effect; neither do I find that it was ever performed by my predecessors to thine."

Lanfranc, who followed the example of his royal master with unfailing complaisance in sacrificing the liberty of the clergy to the king's authority, as well as in disregarding papal admonitions, was succeeded by Anselm in 1093 A.D.

Anselm was born at Aosta, a city of Piedmont, in 1033 A.D., of noble parents, and was one of the most remarkable men of his age. The influence of his gentle and pious mother induced him, when fifteen years old, to apply for admission into a monastery. On his mother's death he was led into dissipation by the profligate example of his father; but later on his old desire regained its ascendency, and he assumed the cowl at the monastery of Bec when in his twenty-seventh year.

He was elected Prior of Bec in 1066 A.D., on the

elevation of Lanfranc to be Abbot of Caen, and he held the office until the death of Herluin, the Abbot of Bec, in 1078 A.D. He was then unanimously chosen by the monks to fill the vacant office. "Upon this Anselm threw himself upon the ground, and, with his face towards the earth, sobbed out his petition to the brethren, that they would not force upon him a trust so onerous. Whereupon the brothers followed his example; they also threw themselves upon the ground, and, prostrate on the earth, they implored their prior to have compassion upon the establishment and upon themselves. It was an awkward position in which to carry on a debate, and we must presume that they remained upon the ground until they fell asleep. When they awoke they must have been too much fatigued to proceed further in the business, and, on several occasions, the scene was re-enacted, until at length the petitions of the brethren prevailed" (Hook's "Lives of the Archbishops," vol. ii. p. 178).

The archbishopric of Canterbury remained vacant nearly four years after the death of Lanfranc, and William Rufus, with the high-handed and dishonourable exercise of the royal prerogative which was not unknown in the eleventh century, applied the emoluments to his own purposes. It is said that at one time he was appropriating the revenues of three bishoprics and thirteen abbeys.

After refusing several invitations to visit England, Anselm, towards whom all eyes were turned as the future primate, was at last prevailed upon to visit the Earl of Chester, an old acquaintance, in his illness. The king received Anselm with cordiality, and made him sit at the right hand of the throne, in the place which had always been occupied by Lanfranc. But at the very moment when the appointment to the archbishopric was expected, Anselm drew upon himself the displeasure of the king by upbraiding him for his conduct and attitude towards the Church.

At this juncture William fell ill. Tortured by the superstitions and fears that so frequently assail the evil-doer at such times, he became convinced that his recovery depended on his appointing an archbishop. Anselm happened to be in the neighbourhood, and was sent for. He did his work faithfully as a priest of God by admonition and reproof. The king expressed repentance, and promised amendment of life and conduct. When asked by those who stood by his sick-bed, "Who is to be the primate?" he replied, "The Abbot of Bec."

The decision was received with cries of delight, and the bishops proceeded with all speed to Anselm, that he might receive the crosier from the king's hand. To their amazement he refused to accompany them, declining the archbishopric on the ground of age, of incapacity for administration, and of his inability to leave the monastery. They would listen to no excuses, but dragged him hurriedly into the royal presence. The scene which then took place is so incredible that, were it not for the circumstantial details, and the assurance of the accuracy of the narrative by one who was an eye-witness, we should hesitate to give credence to the story.

William, now fully persuaded that his life depended on Anselm's appointment to the see, entreated him, with tears in his eyes, to deliver him from the deadly peril in which he stood. The new archbishop still resisted, whereupon the king commanded all who were present to fling themselves at the abbot's feet, and implore him to have pity on their dying master. As he showed some signs of relenting, there was a cry of "The crosier, the crosier!" This was placed in the king's hand while Anselm was dragged towards the bed. He immediately placed his hands in his pockets, but the bishops forced them out; some held down his left hand, while others seized his right hand and brought it in contact with that of the king. But the fist was firmly closed and would not open. At length the forefinger gave way, and in a moment the crosier was placed between the finger and thumb, and the hand clasped. No sooner was this accomplished, than a shout went up, "Long live the new archbishop!" He was carried on the shoulders of the bishops to the nearest church; the *Te Deum* was commenced; and as they marched in procession, the building being filled with an enthusiastic congregation, the archbishop-elect, murmuring the words, "It is nought, it is nought that ye do," fainted away. In a letter to the monks of Bec, he says, "It would have been difficult to make out whether madmen were dragging along one in his senses, or sane men a madman, save that they were chanting, and I, pale with amazement and pain, looked more like one dead than alive."

As a condition of his acceptance of the primacy, Anselm stipulated: first, that the property of the see should be restored in full, and that if any dispute should arise as to what did, or did not, belong to the Church, there should be a legal investigation; secondly, that the king should receive the archbishop as his adviser in all things pertaining to the Church, and regard him as his spiritual father; and thirdly, that he (Anselm) should be at liberty to regard Urban as the pope (Clement being a rival claimant to the papal chair), although as yet the English nation had been neutral, and had acknowledged neither. The reply of William (who had in the mean time recovered from his illness) to these demands was as follows: "The king is willing to restore the estates which are acknowledged to belong to the Churh; as to the other requirements, he cannot bind himself to any specific promise."

Thus only one concession was made at the time when Anselm accepted the primacy, and we shall see how soon this single pledge was broken.

The new archbishop met the king at Winchester, and did homage, the investiture having already taken place. He was consecrated at Canterbury by the Archbishop of York, assisted by all the bishops save two (who were absent on acount of illness), on December 4, 1093 A.D.

At Christmas he repaired to Gloucester, where the Court was assembled, in order, at the urgent advice of his friends, to make an offering of money to the king, who was in great want. Lest he should be accused of purchasing his position by a simoniacal transaction, he fixed his gift at five hundred marks. At first the king was pleased; but on reflection he considered that the amount should have been double, and the money was returned as insufficient.

An audience was demanded by the primate, at which high words passed between prelate and monarch. This was the commencement of the series of misunderstandings and controversies between them which entailed such misery upon the country; and we cannot but feel that much of the trouble might have been averted if Anselm had acted with more tact and worldly wisdom, and if his performance of his duty, from which, however unpleasant, he never shrank, had been, so far as his intercourse with William was concerned, less ill-timed, unfortunate, and injudicious.

The friction was increased, and the relationship further strained, by the archbishop's request for the holding of a synod, to consider the spiritual destitution of the country, and the low state of morals. The king listened impatiently for some time, and then exclaimed, "Enough; talk to me no more about it." Anselm then proceeded to censure his royal master for keeping so many of the abbeys without abbots, thus causing demoralization among the monks, and for his backwardness in redressing these and other evils. The abbeys referred to were exempt from episcopal jurisdiction; the king, therefore, turned fiercely upon the archbishop, exclaiming, "What is that to you? Are not the abbeys mine? You do what you will with your own, and surely I may do what I will with mine."

A year later, the king returned from a military expedition in Normandy, which had been a failure. Anselm applied to him for permission to visit Rome for the purpose of receiving the pallium from the pope. "From which pope?" asked William.

"From Urban," was the reply. It will be remembered that when Anselm had previously raised this question William had evaded it. The evident anticipation of the royal decision by one of his subjects roused the indignation of the king. "Urban," he said, "I have not acknowledged. By my customs, by the customs of my father, no man may acknowledge a pope in England without my leave. To challenge my power in this is as much as to deprive me of my crown."

The archbishop, nothing daunted, demanded that the question at issue should be investigated by a council of the chief men in Church and State. The meeting was accordingly convened, and took place on March 11, 1095 A.D. The king was not present. Anselm opened the proceeding by complaining that he was reduced to the dilemma of either forfeiting his fealty to the king, or of renouncing his obedience to the pope. The bishops replied, declining to enter into the religious question, and urging the primate to make unconditional submission to the sovereign, as an atonement for what they considered to have been the usurpation of the royal prerogative. After a protracted discussion, the meeting dispersed without any result, and the matter was allowed to drop.

While Anselm returned to his devotions and his studies, the king was employing himself in efforts for the humiliation of the archbishop. Having found, through trusted ambassadors who had been despatched to Rome, that Urban was the most pliable of the rival popes, he arranged that the pallium should be sent to himself, instead of to the primate, and then issued a proclamation, without consultation or communication with Anselm, acknowledging Urban as pope. Through the consummate diplomacy of Walter, Bishop of Albano, the papal legate, a reconciliation was effected between the archbishop and the king; and on the appointed day the pallium was placed by the legate on the altar of Canterbury Cathedral, whence it was removed by Anselm, who placed it on his own shoulders with great ceremony.

The next subject of disagreement between the primate and the king was the desire of the former to visit the pope for the purpose of obtaining counsel and advice, and the determination of the latter to prevent him from taking this step. The king commanded him under no circumstances to appeal to the see of St. Peter or his vicar. He was well aware that Anselm's object was to concert measures with the pope by which he might evade his promise to adhere to the laws and customs of England. The archbishop refused compliance with the command, and in spite of the warnings and entreaties of the bishops, adhered to his resolution to make the journey, although he had been informed that the consequence of such an act would be the forfeiture of his position and possessions. He paid a visit to William. "Not knowing when I may see you again," said the archbishop, "I now, as a spiritual father to a son, offer you my benediction, if you do not reject it." "Your benediction," replied the king, "I do not reject;" whereupon he bowed his head, and Anselm with his right hand made over him the sign of the cross. They never met again.

The archbishop left England in October, 1097 A.D., and gradually made his way to Rome. The difficulties of the journey were increased by the fact that when he sojourned at places where Urban was recognized as pope, he was received as a saint and confessor; while in those provinces which acknowledged Clement, the saint became a schismatic, and was obliged to travel in disguise. The story of the procrastination and dilatory proceedings of Urban in considering the mutual attitude of the King of England and the Archbishop of Canterbury towards each other is too complicated to be here told in detail. The pope was a thorough politician; and while it served his purpose to affect a feeling of indignation, it would have been a suicidal act of impolicy at the time to break with William. At length Anselm realized that Urban had no intention of assisting him, and consequently left Rome.

Shortly after, in August, 1100 A.D., Anselm received the intelligence of the death of the king. He was visibly affected, as any good man would be on hearing of the sudden death of a bad man, cut off in the midst of his sins. At Lyons he found a monk from Canterbury, who, in the name of the mother Church of England, required his immediate return. He received a cordial invitation from King Henry, who undertook to abolish all the abuses and enormities of the preceding reign, and, restoring freedom to the Church, to fill up without delay all vacancies in spiritual offices, and not to appropriate their revenues for his own advantage. On Anselm's arrival in England he was welcomed by the king with every demonstration of reverence and respect.

Soon, however, a new controversy arose. Henry, anxious to show the sincerity of his promise to restore the forfeited property of the Church of Canterbury by reinstating Anselm, made arrangements for his investiture. To the surprise of all, the archbishop refused to receive investiture at the hands of the king, a layman.

It will be necessary to examine briefly the history of this question. Under Canute England had accepted the old continental rule that the sovereign should invest ecclesiastics with the temporalities of their benefices by the transfer of certain symbols, which, in the case of a bishop, consisted of a staff and ring. On the establishment of the feudal system, the Church everywhere began to look upon this ancient ceremony with suspicion. The feeling grew that its continuance would render the Church too dependent upon the civil ruler. Moreover, it was argued that, inasmuch as the staff and ring symbolized to some extent the spiritual powers of the episcopate, and these were not derived from earthly sovereignties, the investiture by the king was misleading. During the pontificate of Gregory VII., by a synod held at Rome in 1075 A.D., ecclesiastics were expressly forbidden to receive any investiture from the hands of an emperor, a king, or any lay person.

Anselm appears to have been ignorant of this ruling until his visit to Rome, and this accounts for his having accepted investiture at the hands of William, though he now declined to receive it from Henry, and refused to consecrate the bishops whom the king had invested.

While Lanfranc had been an imperialist, asserting the independence of the Church of England, Anselm was a papist, desiring its amalgamation with the Church of Rome.

Although advanced in years, he again undertook the journey to Rome, in order to ascertain clearly the ruling of Pope Paschal, who had succeeded Urban in the papal see. But the pope, although without the slightest intention of sanctioning lay investiture, had no wish to quarrel with the English king. By means of judiciously worded letters to both parties, apparently taking the side of each in the controversy, he avoided coming to any decision.

The dispute was ultimately settled at a council held at the king's palace in London, in 1107 A.D., when it was resolved: (1) That for the future no one should be invested by the king or any lay hand in any bishopric or abbey by the delivering of a pastoral staff or a ring; (2) That no one elected to any prelacy should be denied consecration on account of the homage he does to the king.

In 1108 A.D. Anselm presided at a synod held in London, which passed a series of stringent regulations for enforcing the celibacy of the clergy.

After a protracted illness, he died on April 21, 1109 A.D., in the seventy-sixth year of his age, and was buried in Canterbury Cathedral.

He was the author of a considerable number of devotional and doctrinal works. Some among them, notably his "Meditations," have been translated more than once, and are still in the hands of pious persons of almost every school of theology.

His character was that of an earnest and deeply religious man. While ostensibly contending for the liberties of the Church, he was, in reality, endeavouring to supersede a royal by a spiritual despotism; to substitute the authority of the Pope of Rome for that of the King of England. In the contemplative life, the virtues and the graces of Anselm were such as to procure for him the admiration and respect of the Church in every age; but as a practical man he failed. And yet the single-mindedness, gentleness, large-heartedness, and piety which he displayed in so conspicuous a degree, combine to render him one of the brightest ornaments of the Christian Church.

CHAPTER IV.

THOMAS À BECKET (1162-1171 A.D.).

THE period of fifty-three years from the death of Anselm to the accession of Becket is chiefly notable on account of the persistent, and to a great extent successful, efforts on the part of the papacy to establish a spiritual supremacy over the Church of England. For this consummation William de Corbeuil, nicknamed by the monks "Old Turmoil," who was primate from 1123 A.D. to 1136 A.D., was mainly responsible. He was the first Archbishop of Canterbury who acknowledged himself to be simply a deputy of the pope in this country. For nearly four hundred years after his death, until 1531 A.D., the Church of England, although the authority of the Bishop of Rome was never acknowledged by her in her councils, continued to struggle and writhe under the powerful dominion which the popes, with the frequent assistance of the monarch, were enabled to exercise and assert.

The year 1115 A.D. is of interest because of the union which took place between the English and Welsh Churches. The Church of Wales, the surviving portion of the ancient British Church, was henceforth amalgamated with the English Church, forming one religious body instead of two bodies in communion with one another. This was accomplished through the Welsh bishops consenting to take the oath of canonical obedience to the Archbishop of Canterbury, and recognizing him as their metropolitan.

Theobald succeeded William de Corbeuil, holding office for two and twenty years, until his death in 1161 A.D. It was to his advice and influence that the young king, Henry II., who came to the throne of this country after the disgraceful misrule by Stephen, gathered round him a number of earnest men who helped him to govern his people with more justice and wisdom than his predecessor had shown. Chief among these was Thomas Becket, who had been for some time confidential secretary to the Archbishop of Canterbury.

Thomas, the son of Gilbert Becket, a famous merchant and citizen of London, was born at his father's house in Cheapside, on December 21, 1118 A.D., and was baptized in St. Mary Cole Church.

On leaving school, where, without becoming a scholar in the technical sense of the word, he had acquired the art, so important in those days, of speaking Latin fluently, the youthful Thomas was admitted into the household of Richer de l'Aigle, a great noble, at Pevensey Castle, in order that he might be initiated into the arts of chivalry, and learn the other accomplishments of the age.

When he was twenty-one years old his mother died, and shortly afterwards he determined to complete his studies in the schools of Paris.

In 1142 A.D. he was introduced to Theobald, Archbishop of Canterbury, and obtained an appointment in his household. In those days it was necessary for a successful career that a man should be either a knight or a cleric. Becket's aversion to theological studies, and his natural inclination towards secular pursuits, prevented him for a time from seeking ordination. At length he was admitted to the minor orders of the Church, not that he might perform any clerical duties, but simply that a sufficient income might be secured to him. He became Rector of St. Mary-le-Strand, and of Otford in Kent. When Roger became Archbishop of York in 1154 A.D., Thomas, though only a deacon, was appointed to succeed him as Archdeacon of Canterbury, the most lucrative office, next to a bishopric, in the Church.

On the accession of Henry II., Thomas the archdeacon was removed, at the instance of Theobald himself, from the court of the archbishop to that of the king, and became "Thomas the Chancellor," as he describes himself in the charters which still exist.

At the present time, when the pressure of work is so severe and so varied in all the three orders of the ministry, it sounds strange to read of ecclesiastics holding high office in the State. But for many centuries this was the rule rather than the exception; and the principle holds good even now, when the two Archbishops and the Bishop of London, besides being members of the House of Lords, are by virtue of their office "sworn of" Her Majesty's Privy Council.

The career of Thomas the Chancellor was a career of uninterrupted brilliancy, and he has been justly included in the catalogue of the most eminent of English statesmen. While maintaining his position with considerable pomp and lavish expenditure, he was always careful to husband his resources, so that he might be able, in time of war, to render the king effectual service, or, at his own cost, to conduct an expensive diplomatic mission. For example, when the war of Toulouse commenced, he provided and rode at the head of seven hundred fully equipped knights; clad, not in cope or surplice, but in helm and cuirass. Again, when he undertook the celebrated embassy to France in 1159 A.D., to seek in marriage the French king's daughter, aged three months, for King Henry's son, who was three years her senior, he both evinced his patriotism and indulged his own taste for magnificence. As he passed through the cities of France, the entire population turned out to behold the procession. His object in all this was not to gratify his personal vanity, but to impress the neighbours of England with a sense of the importance of her ruler; a thought that found expression in the words, "If such be the King of England's chancellor, what manner of man must the King of England himself be!"

In April, 1161 A.D., Archbishop Theobald died. Henry and Becket were at the time in Normandy, and as the chancellor was taking leave of the king, in order to return to England on political business, Henry informed him that he was to be the new Archbishop of Canterbury. Believing that the king was speaking in jest, he pointed to his gay attire, as indicative of his secular tastes and habits, and replied, "A pretty saint you wish to place over that holy bishopric and that famous monastery."

When he found that the king was resolute in his determination, Becket warned him that if the appointment were made it would be the termination of their friendship. He knew Henry, and he knew himself. He understood that the king would expect from an archbishop whom he nominated a compliance with his wishes which the archbishop would feel it his duty to resist.

It is only fair to Becket to state that he never sought the primacy. He must have known that if he outlived Theobald, the archbishopric would be within his reach. But, as chancellor, he was in the very sphere adapted to his talents and inclinations, while he had never shown any predilection for the religious life of an ecclesiastic. If his ambition had led him to covet the position, he would, while chancellor, have taken some pains to conciliate the various parties whose consents were required before a valid election could take place. On the contrary, he was regarded by many of the bishops as "a despiser of the clergy," and was declared to be a "persecutor and destroyer of Holy Church."

More than a year elapsed before the king could carry his point, during which time Becket maintained a dignified attitude, neither canvassing for the appointment, nor opposing Henry's wishes. He was ordained to the priesthood by his friend Walter, Bishop of Rochester, on the eve of Whitsunday,

1162 A.D.; and was consecrated, eight days after, by Henry de Blois, Bishop of Winchester.

The first act of the new archbishop was to appoint the day of his consecration, the octave of Whitsunday, to form a festival in the Church of England, in honour of the Holy and Undivided Trinity. From that day to this, the festival of Trinity Sunday has been thus observed in this country. The Roman Church followed the example of the Anglican Church by adopting the festival in the fourteenth century.

Becket immediately resigned the chancellorship, and in many ways showed himself determined to put an end to his friendship with Henry. For upwards of twelve months the king, contrary to his natural disposition, evinced an anxiety to retain the affection of his former comrade. But the attitude of the latter made it inevitable that the breach between them must occur sooner or later.

A year after his consecration, the archbishop attended the Council of Tours, where the magnificence and pomp with which he surrounded himself outshone that of the pope. His proposal, which, however, was not acted upon, that Anselm should be canonized (this was not done till three centuries later), and the tone which prevailed at the council, due in great measure to his influence, against the exercise of secular authority, convinced the king that he would be compelled to make a firm stand on behalf of the supremacy of the Crown. The action of the archbishop, on his return, in setting the laws of William the Conqueror at defiance by excommunicating William of Eynesford, who was tenant-in-chief of the Crown, for refusing to present a nominee of the archbishop's to a living of which he was patron, further incensed Henry.

From the day when he was appointed to the primacy, Becket determined, at all costs, to maintain the power of the Church against the royal encroachment. It is not surprising that, before long, two men, so masterful, and each contending for what he considered a vital principle, should come into active collision. This occurred at a council held by the king at Woodstock, when he proposed that the Danegeld, a payment made to the local sheriffs, should become a compulsory tax levied by the Crown. The king was so enraged that his former chancellor should oppose his wishes, that he shouted out, "By God's eyes, the money shall be paid as revenue." Whereupon Becket retorted, "And by God's eyes, while I live, from land of mine no such payment shall be made."

The next point of dispute which arose was the right, which the king desired to establish, of trying the clergy in civil courts for criminal charges. The separation between the civil and ecclesiastical courts, which had been effected by William the Conqueror, resulted in the practical immunity of the worst class of clerical offenders from adequate punishment. A great council was convened at Westminster, in October, 1163 A.D., to determine the matter. The king, in a temperate speech, requested that any of the clergy, convicted in the spiritual courts of robbery, murder, or other crimes, should be delivered over to the officers of the royal courts to be dealt with according to the laws of the land. The bishops at first assented; but, won over by the impassioned eloquence of Becket, who raised his **favourite** cry, "The liberty of the Church!" they declared that it was inconsistent with their duty to the Church to give an unqualified consent to the demand. Henry then inquired if the bishops would conform, unreservedly, to the usages of his kingdom, and the royal constitutions of his ancestors. Becket readily replied, "We will, in all things, saving our order." The king demanded the withdrawal of the qualifying phrase, and angrily retired. A subsequent interview between him **and** the archbishop **only served to** embitter their relations.

Becket immediately wrote to the pope for advice. As usual, unwilling to lose the friendship of the English king, the Bishop of Rome urged that concessions should be made for the sake of peace. The archbishop, finding himself deserted in a quarter where he looked for support, and learning that the majority of the bishops regarded him as being in error, capitulated. He went to the king, and promised **to** omit **the phrase which** had given **such** dire offence.

Henry required that the withdrawal should be public, and summoned a council to meet at the Castle of Clarendon, near Salisbury, in January, 1164 A.D. Two archbishops and eleven bishops were present. The council proceeded to draw up sixteen articles, called the "Constitutions of Clarendon," **the** object of which was to restrain the authority of the Church, and make the clergy amenable to the civil courts. They contained no absolutely novel enactments, but merely reaffirmed the ancient principle of the Realm and Church **of** England, in opposition to the growing Romanizing tendencies. They were, however, somewhat stringent in their provisions.

Becket refused to accept the Constitutions, and was supported in his refusal by the bishops. The king was furious, and for a time there was danger of an outburst of violence on the part of the barons, who favoured the royal demand.

Suddenly, however, for no reason that has ever been assigned, the archbishop's resolution gave way. He acted, for the only time in his life, with weakness and inconsistency. Returning to the bishops, he said, "It is God's will that I should perjure myself; for the present I submit and incur perjury, to repent of it hereafter as I best may."

The king, as may be imagined, was delighted when the archbishop and his suffragans came and declared their assent to the Constitutions; but was amazed and irritated when Becket, on being requested to affix his official seal to the document, exclaimed, "By God Almighty! never, while there is breath in my body, shall seal of mine touch them."

The next move, on the part of the king, was to call a council at Northampton, in 1164 A.D., at which Becket was accused of perjury, contempt of the Crown, and misappropriation of funds during his chancellorship (although, when he resigned the office, he received an express declaration of his discharge from all secular obligations); and he was condemned to forfeit all his estates and possessions to the king. On the recommendation of Henry de Blois, he offered two thousand marks as indemnity, which the king, whose object was to humiliate and crush the primate, refused to accept. At a later session of the council, Becket was impeached for high treason, and the Earl of Leicester, as chief justice, called upon him to hear his sentence. "Nay, son earl," was the reply, "first hear me. . . . I decline to receive judgment from the king or you, or any other temporal peer, and will be judged under God by the pope alone."

Carrying his cross before him, he left the council chamber with dignity, followed by insults and cries of "Traitor!" He fled for sanctuary to St. Andrew's Church, whence, under cover of night, he proceeded to Lincoln, journeying through Eastry, and at length arrived at Sandwich. He landed on the French coast at Gravelines, and assumed the disguise of a Cistercian monk, until he reached St. Omer, where he was hospitably entertained. On arriving at Soissons, he resumed his state as Archbishop of Canterbury, and proceeded to visit the pope at Sens, escorted by three hundred knights.

Meanwhile, Henry had despatched envoys to the pope, desiring that "the traitor" should be sent back to England, and that a special legate should be appointed to investigate the charges against him. The course taken by the Bishop of Rome, of appearing to side with both disputants, and in reality favouring neither, gave offence to each. Becket thereupon played his master-stroke. Drawing the archiepiscopal ring from his finger, he handed it to the pope, and resigned the see of Canterbury into his hands, praying him to appoint a worthy successor. Next day the ring was returned to the archbishop, who was thus able afterwards to say that he held the primacy from the pope and not from the king.

On St. Andrew's Day, 1164 A.D., Becket arrived at Pontigny, where he remained for nearly two years, during which time he devoted himself to self-discipline, and meditation on sacred subjects.

Henry, having confiscated the archbishop's property, proceeded to display his vindictiveness by issuing a decree of banishment and exile against all the relations of Becket, male and female, his clerks, dependants, friends and servants. Four hundred individuals, impoverished and starving, were cast on a foreign coast in the depth of winter, and with infinite difficulty made their way to Pontigny, where, through the kindness of the French king and the generosity of the French people, the archbishop, himself an exile and dependent on the charity of others, was enabled to procure for them the necessaries of life.

The contest between Henry and Becket waged with continued bitterness, in spite of all efforts on the part of Pope Alexander to mediate, for several years. At length, on the Feast of Epiphany, 1169 A.D., a conference on political affairs between the kings of England and France, held on the plains of Montmirail, near Chartres, was taken advantage of for effecting a reconciliation. Henry was in a generous mood, and desired that all past subjects of dispute should be swept aside. Becket undertook to submit himself to the king, "saving God's honour." These words had before incensed Henry, as implying a disregard of God's honour on his own part. At the earnest solicitation of his friends, the archbishop made an unconditional surrender; and just as a shout of joy went up at this happy termination of the long-protracted struggle, Becket added the obnoxious sentence, and thus destroyed all hope of peace. As the archbishop returned to Sens, he was encouraged by the acclamations of the populace, who gave him an ovation, praising him as the man that "defied two kings for the honour of his God."

A second meeting, later in the year, was held at Montmartre, near Paris. By dint of great exertions on the part of Vivian, the papal envoy, to smooth over difficulties, promises were obtained from both disputants that each would abstain from usurping the other's prerogatives, and a reconciliation was effected. Becket's ill-advised demand for entire restitution of all the property of which he and his followers had been deprived, valued by him at thirty thousand marks, was received calmly by the king, who undertook to act fairly in the matter. Before separating with renewed cordiality, as all those present earnestly hoped, the archbishop approached Henry to offer the kiss of peace. Impelled, apparently, by a desire to renew the quarrel, he used the words which he knew would enrage the king, "I kiss you to the honour of God," and a second time the attempt to bring them together proved a failure.

A third meeting took place at Freteval, between Chartres and Tours, where all enmity was for the time buried. Henry conceded everything, even going so far as to say, "Why is it that you will not do as I wish? I would put everything into your hands."

After considerable delay, occasioned by making

preparations for returning to England with the dignity and state befitting his office, Becket landed at Sandwich. He had carried all his points. A proud king had succumbed before him; the "Constitutions of Clarendon" were virtually suspended; his advent was awaited with eagerness. Yet it was with sad misgivings that he made the journey. He doubted the good faith of Henry; he knew that he had many enemies, including some godless and unscrupulous ruffians; and it was with something of a prophetic foresight that he said, as he bade farewell to the Bishop of Paris, "I go to England to die."

From Canterbury the archbishop, who rejoiced in popular demonstration, made a series of triumphal processions to London, but was warned by the young prince to return.

Henry was at the time staying at Bayeux, where he was joined by the prelates from England whom Becket had excommunicated. In one of his mad fits of anger he exclaimed, "Of the caitiffs who eat my bread, are there none to free me of this turbulent priest?"

Four of the knights who stood by, desperate characters, immediately returned to England. Their names were Reginald Fitzurse, William de Tracy, Hugh de Morville, and Richard Brito.

They found their way into Becket's palace at Canterbury, and a stormy interview took place. He defied them to do their worst, and after an exhibition of almost insane fury, they rushed out of the chamber, but soon returned with their weapons and clad in armour. His friends dragged the archbishop by force into the cathedral, where vespers had just commenced. Becket forbade the monks to bar the cloister doors, and his enemies were upon him in a moment. Their object was not to murder him, but to take him prisoner. He resisted with might and main, and shook off his assailants with almost incredible strength. The first blow he received was from Fitzurse. This was immediately followed by a terrific sword-stroke on the head from De Tracy. Bowing himself, he ejaculated, "I commend my soul to God, to St. Denys, and the saints of the Church." As he grew weaker from loss of blood, he cried, "Lord, into Thy hands I commend my spirit." A final blow from Richard Brito consummated the murder, the force with which it was struck being so great that the sword was broken by contact with the marble pavement.

The murderers, after ransacking the palace, fled. The monks, on their return, found the dead body of the archbishop, which was laid in state on the high altar, and buried the following day in the crypt of the cathedral.

Becket was a brave man, with considerable nobility of character, which was marred by a perversity and quickness of temper that led him to commit grave errors of judgment. The influence of the man and of the cause for which he strove was enormously enhanced by the brutality of his murder, and the fact that it was committed within the sacred precincts of the cathedral.

CHAPTER V.

HENRY CHICHELEY (1414–1443 A.D.).

THE murder of Thomas à Becket sent a thrill of horror through the civilized world. King Henry felt that his rash words had given a certain authorization for the commission of the crime, and bitterly repented his hasty utterance. When he returned to England in 1174 A.D., "he rode from Southampton to Canterbury without resting, dismounted at the gate of the city, walked barefoot through the streets to the cathedral, and prostrated himself on the ground before the tomb. In the chapter-house he caused each of the monks to strike him with the 'discipline,' and afterwards he spent the whole night in the church beside the tomb."

The chief consequences, however, of Becket's death were the complete surrender on the part of the king of everything for which he had been contending, and an accession of strength to the papal claims over the Anglican Church.

The struggle between national ecclesiastical independence and presumptuous papal aggrandizement was unintermittent. The balance of power rested largely in the hands of our kings, who at one moment supported the pope in the hopes of bending the bishops and clergy to their will, and at another resented the interference of the Bishop of Rome as trenching on their rights and prerogatives.

A dispute of some importance arose during the primacy of Archbishop Baldwin as to the election of bishops. In Anglo-Saxon days the clergy of each diocese had the privilege of choosing their ecclesiastical superiors, except in the case of the Archbishop of Canterbury, who was usually elected by the monks and canons of that cathedral, the king, owing to the importance of the appointment, exercising considerable influence over their choice. From the time of the Norman Conquest it became the custom for the king to nominate the occupants of episcopal sees. After the murder of Becket, the bishops of the province of Canterbury claimed a voice in the election of their primate, and a compromise was accordingly effected by which the king issued a *congé d'élire*, or leave to elect, to the chapters, and their choice was submitted to him for ratification and approval. The present system, which is merely a slight modification of the above, allows the Crown to nominate, and the Dean and Chapter then proceed to the election of the person named to them.

The Middle Ages witnessed considerable improvements in the relations of the Church to the State. We can trace in succession the far-reaching reforms within the Church effected by Hugh of Lincoln (1186-1200 A.D.), and Grossetête, Bishop of Lincoln (1235-1253 A.D.); the signing of Magna Charta by King John in 1215 A.D., the first clause of which runs as follows: "That the Church of England shall be free, and hold her rights entire, and her liberties inviolate;" the meeting of Parliament, when for the first time the representatives of the citizens and burgesses (*i.e.* the Commons) were summoned to deliberate with the prelates and nobles for the welfare of the country, in 1265 A.D.; the passing of laws resisting the encroachments of the papal see, notably the Statute of Mortmain in 1279 A.D. (forbidding the Church to acquire lands by will); the Statute of Provisors in 1351 A.D. (requiring kings and all other lords to present to benefices of which they are patrons, and not allowing the Bishop of Rome to fill the vacancies); and the Statute of Præmunire in 1353 A.D. (withdrawing the protection of the State from, and confiscating the goods of, all who sued for redress in the papal courts). These last two statutes were made more stringent in 1390 and 1393 A.D. respectively. Of the latter, Bishop Stubbs says that this statute is "the clue to the events that connect the Constitutions of Clarendon with the Reformation."

One of the most powerful factors in preparing for the Reformation was the influence of John de Wycliffe (born 1322 A.D.), who by his writings roused the nation to repudiate the alien oppression of Rome, and by his translation of the Bible enabled men to apprehend the truths of Christianity through the individual study of the sacred records, instead of receiving distorted versions at second-hand from papal sources, which in great measure misled the priests and flock alike.

The abuses in the monastic system led to the suppression of many of the monasteries and convents, and their wealth (in those cases where the treasures were not confiscated by the king) was alienated to the maintenance of poor scholars at the universities. By this means the universities became from that time the centres of scholarship and research.

The revival of religious earnestness and zeal during this period was largely due to the preaching of the mendicant friars. They had their origin in the devotion of two men—St. Dominic, a Spaniard (1170–1221 A.D.), and St. Francis of Assisi in Italy (1182–1226 A.D.). The Dominicans, called in England "Black-friars" (from the colour of their dress), took their name from the former, while the Franciscans, or "Grey-friars," were those founded by the latter. Besides these, there sprang up the Carmelites, or "White-friars," and the "Austin-friars," or Augustinians.

Their preaching infused new life into the Church of England, and brought about a system of evangelizing which was almost unknown to the parochial clergy of their day. They gradually came to enlist the sympathy of the higher classes, in consequence of their untiring and self-denying labours in the lowest and poorest dens of misery and disease. Men of wealth were induced to leave them bequests. The consequence of this change in their habits and condition soon brought about the demoralization of the friars. They became, to a great extent, greedy fortune-hunters, while their zeal for reform spent itself in abuse of the parish priests, and in defending every papal attempt to encroach on the rights and independence of the Church.

Such, in a few words, is the story of the position

of the Anglican Church during the thirteenth and fourteenth centuries.

Archbishop Arundel (1396-1414 A.D.) was succeeded in the primacy by Chicheley. Henry Chicheley, the son of a yeoman of Higham Ferrers, in Northamptonshire, was born in 1362 A.D., and was admitted a scholar of Winchester College in 1373 A.D. After his public school education was completed, Chicheley proceeded to New College, Oxford, of which he became a Fellow. He took his degree, as a Bachelor of Laws, in 1389 A.D.

On May 26, 1396 A.D., he was ordained to the diaconate, and in September of the same year to the priesthood, becoming at the same time Rector of St. Stephen's, Walbrook. In addition to his parochial duties, Chicheley practised as a lawyer, and was successful as an advocate in the Court of Arches. His abilities brought him to the notice of Richard of Mitford, Bishop of Salisbury, who required a legal adviser, and appointed this rising barrister-priest to the office. At this time preferments simply poured in upon Chicheley. He became Archdeacon of Dorset, and a Prebendary of Salisbury in 1397 A.D.; three years later he was made Canon of St. David's; in 1402 A.D. he was appointed Archdeacon of Salisbury; a canonry of Lincoln was given him the following year; in 1404 A.D. he received the chancellorship of Salisbury, with one or two livings.

The fact of his accumulating these preferments is no proof that Chicheley was avaricious. But his ambition, and his desire to take part in the affairs of State, led him to welcome these ecclesiastical appointments, inasmuch as they provided him with the means of serving the king without making demands upon the royal treasury.

His first State appointment was in July, 1406 A.D., when he was sent on a mission, jointly with Sir John Cheyne, to Pope Innocent VII., with a view to the establishment of friendly relations between the English and the papal courts. A few months later he was employed to negotiate a peace between France and England. The following year he was again sent to Rome, on an embassy to Pope Gregory XII., the occupant of the papal chair, who was at that time acknowledged in England, in opposition to his rival. It will be remembered that for thirty years, from the death of Gregory XI. in 1378 A.D., Europe was scandalized by the spectacle of two men, sometimes even of three, assuming to be successors of St. Peter and Vicars of Christ, who hurled against each other the most terrible anathemas, and invoked the horrors of war in the name of the Prince of Peace.

While Chicheley was at the papal court, the news reached him of the death of Guy, Bishop of St. David's. He had received from the king the promise of this see, in the event of its becoming vacant during his absence. He thereupon applied to the pope for consecration, and returned to England on August 28, 1407 A.D., as bishop. Before, however, he could be invested with the spiritualities of the see, he was required to take the oath of canonical obedience to the Archbishop of Canterbury, and to do homage to the king. This precaution was taken lest his consecration by the Bishop of Rome should establish a precedent on the part of the papacy which might in any way prejudice the rights, privileges, or independence of the English Church and realm.

Before he had time to visit his diocese, Chicheley was again requisitioned to attend, as one of the delegates representing the Church of England, the Œcumenical Synod convened to meet at Pisa. Here the corruptions of the Roman Church were unmercifully exposed; the two rival popes were proved to be incorrigible heretics and obstinate schismatics, and were solemnly excommunicated; and Peter Filargo, a Franciscan prior and a native of Candia, was unanimously elected to the papacy as Alexander V.

On his return, Chicheley, desiring to retire from public and diplomatic life, and to devote himself to the spiritual work of his diocese, resigned most of his preferments, feeling that he no longer required, for State purposes, the wealth that they produced. He repaired to St. David's, and was enthroned on May 20, 1411 A.D.

King Henry IV. died in 1413 A.D., and his son, Henry V., immediately summoned the Bishop of St. David's to court, in order that he might supply information as to the precise terms of the late truce with France. The clear-headedness and straightforwardness of the prelate made a great impression on the young king's mind, and from this first interview we may date the lifelong friendship between the two.

In the following year, on the death of Arundel, Henry Chicheley was appointed, amid universal acclamations, to the primacy; the pall being delivered to him by the Bishops of Winchester and Norwich on July 24, 1414 A.D.

The internal condition of England at this time was very unsettled. The insurrection under Sir John Oldcastle was only defeated by the prompt and energetic action of the king. The universal opinion of the royal counsellors, which was shared by the new archbishop, was that the best plan for diminishing the discontent at home would be to prosecute the war with France vigorously, instead of perpetually delaying the settlement of the dispute between the two nations by the renewal of truces which were never kept.

As soon as the determination was arrived at that hostile measures were to be recommenced, Chicheley was both zealous and successful in helping to raise the necessary funds. He obtained from the clergy a subsidy of twopence, which was devoted to the service of the king. He also set the precedent, which was afterwards followed with unsparing severity, of confiscating monastic property for replenishing the State coffers; although under him it was only the possessions of the alien priories that were sold, on the ground that they belonged to foreigners who were hostile to the King of England. The preparations, both for attack and defence, were carried out with the utmost efficiency, the king being especially active and far-seeing. His high opinion of the character and abilities of the archbishop led to his becoming Henry's chief adviser, and subsequently prime minister.

Before the fleet sailed from Southampton, the primate waited upon the king to receive his last commands, and to confer his benediction upon the armament. The news of the safe arrival of the king and his army at the mouth of the Seine, near Honfleur, was awaited with eagerness. On August 18, 1415 A.D., the siege of Harfleur commenced, and on September 22 the town surrendered, and immense booty was secured by the king. But the greatest danger was to come. The troops had been decimated by disease, the fleet had dispersed, and the only means of return was by way of the English town of Calais. To reach it, however, Henry must march through the hostile country of Normandy, where an army of fourteen thousand men was waiting to attack him. The anxiety at home was intense. At length came the joyful news to the archbishop at Lambeth that the battle of Agincourt had been fought and won, notwithstanding that the French outnumbered the English in the proportion of six to one. Chicheley, on whose shoulders had rested a terrible burden of responsibility in the absence of the king, hastened to Canterbury to welcome the victorious monarch. Special thanksgiving services, at each of which Henry was present, were held in Canterbury Cathedral, at St. Paul's, and at Westminster Abbey. The enthusiasm of the people throughout the king's journey was unbounded, and, as he entered London, the crowds hailed him as the conqueror of the national enemy.

We find Chicheley accompanying Henry on the next expedition to France, and he and the Earl of Warwick were deputed to conduct the treaty of surrender with the inhabitants of Rouen. This was signed on January 16, 1419 A.D., and three days later the king made his public entry into the town.

In the following year a treaty of peace between

the two countries was signed, and Henry shortly afterwards married the Princess Katherine, daughter of King Charles VI. of France. To conciliate the conquered nation, the Archbishop of Sens, and not the Archbishop of Canterbury, officiated. Chicheley took the opportunity of using his powers and ability in order to establish peace between the Anglican and Gallican Churches, as well as between the two states. With this object in view, he caused a proclamation to be issued, in which he directed the French to submit to all diocesan ordinances and regulations as they had existed before our conquest of the country, thereby renouncing all claim to jurisdiction on his part. He then returned to England, in order to prepare for the reception of the young queen, and for her coronation.

We find the archbishop at this period acting with great firmness and determination in maintaining the liberties of the Church of England. Acting through his convocation, he availed himself of the schism at Rome to annul all papal immunities and exemptions within his province. He cordially sanctioned, if he did not actually originate, the order in council prohibiting the preferment in England of any foreigner to an ecclesiastical benefice, and in 1421 A.D. he refused a grant to Pope Martin V. when a subsidy was demanded by the papal agent.

It is not, therefore, surprising that the Bishop of Rome should have sought to humiliate Chicheley. He attempted to effect this by proposing to appoint Henry Beaufort, Bishop of Winchester, his legate *à latere*. Beaufort had, at the Council of Constance, materially benefited Pope Martin, and the conferring of a cardinal's hat was the expression of papal gratitude. The archbishop, foreseeing that the effect of the suggested nomination of a legate would practically be to supersede the primate, and to subjugate the Church of England to the Church of Rome, at once wrote to the king an earnest and convincing letter, protesting against this encroachment, and appealing for the withholding of the royal sanction. Henry responded cordially to this request, and refused to permit Beaufort to retain his bishopric if he accepted the cardinalate.

In the death of Henry V., on August 31, 1422 A.D., the archbishop lost a true and sterling friend, and one on whose wisdom, firmness, and courage he had come to lean for support in all the difficulties of his career.

It was not long before the pope recommenced, with greater determination and energy than ever, his efforts to establish a complete sovereignty over the Church of England, and to compel the primate to act as the representative and delegate of the papacy. Martin was specially angry with the "Statute of Præmunire," to which he constantly applied the epithet "execrable." He wrote violent and abusive letters to Chicheley, who, being now an old man in enfeebled health, was intimidated by the fiery Roman bishop. In one of these letters, the pope, reviewing what he considers the unjust laws against the papacy, proves how independent the Church of England had been before his time, and shows that the royal supremacy which Henry VIII. afterwards claimed, was merely the revival of a royal prerogative that only ceased to exist in the fifteenth century. Chicheley took an unwise step when he applied to Parliament, in obedience to the papal demands, for the repeal of the Statutes of Provisors and Præmunire. The Commons, however, were unwilling to give way to the usurping force, and petitioned the king to uphold the rights of the Anglican Church against the papal aggression. The controversy, in one form or another, continued throughout the rest of the archbishop's life, Martin V. having grasped the fact that he could safely aim at effecting, under the weak government of Henry VI., what he had not dared to attempt when Henry V. was king.

We must now, however, turn to the constructive and educational side of the primate's character, for which, rather than for his statesmanship, his memory is respected and venerated.

In 1437 A.D. he purchased some land at Oxford, on which he founded and built, at his own expense, the College of All Souls. He did not rest until he had provided sufficient endowment to ensure its permanence. He was also the second founder of St. John's College, in the same university.

Nor did he, in the days of his prosperity and magnificence, forget the birthplace from which he had gone forth to attain to the highest position in the Church, and, after the royal family, in the State. He left many marks of his munificent spirit in the little town of Higham Ferrers, rebuilding the parish church, and founding a college of priests.

At Canterbury he spent large sums of money in the adornment of the cathedral, and, in addition to this, he founded the cathedral library, which he furnished with a large collection of books.

The name of Archbishop Chicheley will always be associated with the magnificent historic structure of Lambeth Palace, in consequence of his having built what is perhaps the most interesting portion of the whole range. In the "steward's accounts," preserved at the palace, we find a record of the expenditure on the "Water Tower," which has latterly but erroneously been termed the "Lollards' Tower." The date of its completion was 1435 A.D. The ground floor of this tower, on the same level as the chapel, is called the "Post-room." The post, from which the chamber derives its name, is not, as tradition has so persistently maintained, a relic of mediæval barbarism, proving that heretics were habitually tortured there, but is merely a stay required to prop up a failing beam of unusual span, probably introduced in the beginning of last century. It was down the steps which led from the Post-room to the river that Anne Boleyn passed, on her way to the Tower, after the sentence of divorce had been passed upon her by Cranmer. Another feature of interest in the "Water Tower" is the prison. This, again, has been graphically depicted as a weapon in the hands of cruel archbishops wherewith to persecute the hapless Lollards. Nothing is further from the truth. The prison existed at the primate's palace originally for the incarceration of those condemned to punishment by the archbishops in their capacity as judges, and subsequently as a place of refuge, in which the occupants of the palace protected those who had been unjustly accused for their religious beliefs.

Two excellent portraits of Chicheley are preserved

at Lambeth. One is on glass, preserved in the north-west window of Juxon's Hall, the present library. It is a work of considerable beauty, with the finish of a miniature painting, and is remarkable for the unusually youthful character of the face. The other hangs in the "Guard-room" of the palace, and is believed to be a faithful likeness. It represents him in the act of pronouncing the benediction.

On April 12, 1443 A.D., the good old primate breathed his last, at the age of eighty-one. His remains were deposited in a vault on the north side of the presbytery in Canterbury Cathedral. There, upon a monument erected in his lifetime, reposes his effigy, in the carved magnificence of his pontifical vestments.

With Henry Chicheley the long line of independent archbishops, who had come down in regular succession from Augustine, terminated. They had governed the Church of England, not as delegates from any foreign power, but by their own authority, in spite of the aggressions of the papacy. From this period until the days of Queen Elizabeth the claims of the Bishops of Rome to exercise sovereignty over the Anglican Church, although never admitted by the synods, were frequently conceded under protest, especially when, to suit his own purposes, the king allied himself to the pope, and enforced the papal pretensions by means of royal authority.

Archbishop Chicheley was a powerful statesman, and a deeply spiritual prelate. Though not a Luther, he desired to be, in the highest sense of the word, "a reformer of the corruptions and abuses which were in his day debasing and weakening the Church."

CHAPTER VI.

WILLIAM WARHAM (1503–1532 A.D.).

THE progress of the Church was terribly hindered by the long-continued Wars of the Roses, which extended throughout the greater part of the fifteenth century. At the conclusion of the war, Henry VII. (the founder of the Tudor dynasty) encouraged, rather than opposed, the claims of the Bishops of Rome to absolute ecclesiastical supremacy in England. This brought matters towards the crisis which shortly afterwards resulted in the final overthrow of Roman influence in this country during the following reign.

A definite scheme for raising the intellectual standard of the clergy, and bringing about a reformation in education and scholarship, was formed in Oxford by three friends—Colet, son of a Lord Mayor of London, whose lectures on Holy Scripture, in which he freely condemned the superstitions of the day, attained a remarkable popularity and fame, and who subsequently became Dean of St. Paul's; Erasmus, a poor scholar of Rotterdam, who came to England at the age of thirty, introduced the study of Greek into the universities, subsequently becoming professor of that language at Cambridge, and produced the first Greek Testament ever printed; and Sir Thomas More, who afterwards became Lord High Chancellor. We have in the action of these three men the foundation-stone of the Reformation.

The enormous influence of Thomas Wolsey, Archbishop of York, Lord Chancellor, cardinal, and papal legate, which he exerted in the most powerful manner towards the suppression of abuses in the monastic system and in other ways, gave great impetus to the movement.

Such was the condition of Church affairs in England at the commencement of the reign of Henry VIII., when William Warham was primate.

But, first of all, it will be instructive to inquire what were the various internal causes of the great change that passed over the Church of England in the sixteenth century. They were partly social, partly political, but in the main religious. The Reformation, which was finally effected by the resumption of the royal supremacy in the Act of 1534 A.D., and the decision of Convocation in the same year (subsequently ratified by Act of Parliament), that "the Pope of Rome hath no greater jurisdiction conferred on him by God in Holy Scripture, in this kingdom of England, than any other foreign bishop."

The royal supremacy had existed in theory, if not always in practice, from the earliest days of the monarchy in this country, and therefore the statute referred to above was not the promulgation of a new law, but the reaffirmation of an existing one. Similarly, the rejection of papal authority was merely the enforcement of the principle on which the Church had acted since the days when Hildebrand claimed both temporal and spiritual sovereignty over the whole world, viz. the resistance of any and every attempt to place the Anglican Church in a position of subjection to the Roman. On frequent occasions, when the king, to gain his own personal ends, threw into the scale the weight of his power and influence, the Church was compelled, under protest, to submit for a time to the authority of the papacy; but when this was the case she never rested until she had repelled the usurpation. Under Henry VIII. she happened to be supported by the king in her resistance to Roman aggression, not because that monarch favoured the Reformation, but on account of his personal quarrel with the pope on the subject of his matrimonial alliances.

The corruption and vice which had marked so large a number of the Bishops of Rome during the Middle Ages produced a feeling of disgust and contempt in the minds of all thoughtful men, and prepared them for the furtherance of any scheme which would overthrow, once and for ever, the authority over English ecclesiastical matters which was so repeatedly claimed by the occupants of the papal chair.

The revival of learning, and the facilities (which were daily becoming greater) of studying the Scriptures in the vernacular, unmasked the various legends and falsifications of history, which were so sedulously circulated by those who favoured the attempt to bring about the Roman supremacy, and led men to grasp the fact that the branch of the Catholic Church which arrogated to itself the first place in the visible kingdom of Christ on earth had, by its modern innovations, fallen away from apostolic simplicity.

Thus it came to pass that the Reformation was a practical movement. There was no sudden revolution, no uprooting of cherished beliefs, nor was there the enforcement of strange and unpalatable dogmas upon an unwilling priesthood. This is proved by the almost unanimous voice of the clergy in welcoming the change.

In the present day, when the recent Catholic revival has led us to appreciate and value much of the primitive doctrine and ritual of the Church, which had, until fifty years ago, been lost sight of and well-nigh lost since the sixteenth century, it is the fashion with many people to lay the blame upon those who were responsible for the Reformation. But we must remember that the result of the movement was the outcome of a compromise. The aim of Warham, Cranmer, and Parker, and of those who acted with them, was to preserve the continuity of the Anglican Church. Arrayed against them was the enormous power of the papacy, resisting any attempt at reform, and bent on establishing a permanent supremacy over the Church in this land. Equally formidable and dangerous was the influence of the foreign Protestants, Lutherans, Calvinists, and Zwinglians, who sought the co-operation of England in sweeping aside all trace of Catholicity, and the formation of a sect. Thus our Reformers had to decide how far they could go in abolishing, or at all events in discontinuing non-essentials in teaching and practice, in order that by sacrificing what was not of vital importance they might retain the cardinal truths of the faith, and the apostolical succession, the primitive celebration of the Holy Sacraments, and the like. Regarding the matter with the impartial mind of the student of history, we cannot but feel that, bitterly as the Church has suffered during the intervening period, her apostolic character might have been altogether lost had it not been for the sagacity of those who have been so often abused, guided and overruled, as we may feel sure they were, by the Divine Spirit, in accordance with the parting promise of the risen Lord.

We now come to consider the history of the Archbishop of Canterbury who was privileged to take part in the first efforts towards emancipating the Anglican Church from the thraldom of Rome. William Warham was born at Walsanger, in the county of Southampton, about the year 1450 A.D., and was educated at Winchester. After a distinguished career at Oxford, he came to London in 1488 A.D., and practised with considerable ability as a lawyer in the Court of Arches. He appears to have been ordained in 1493 A.D., and though the dates of his early preferments are uncertain, he was successively Incumbent of Horwood Magna, in the county of Lincoln, and Rector of Barley, in Hertfordshire. His appointment as Precentor of Wells (for the sake of its emoluments) preceded by only a few months his accession to the Mastership of the Rolls, which took place in February, 1494 A.D.

Two years later he was collated to the Archdeaconry of Huntingdon, the duties of which were, as frequently happened, performed by deputy.

For the next few years we find Warham engaged in various diplomatic appointments, the most important of which was the commission empowered to treat with De Puebla about the marriage of Prince Arthur (eldest son of Henry VII.) and Katharine of Arragon.

He was made Bishop of London in 1501 A.D., being consecrated in the following year. Before taking possession of the see he resigned the office of Master of the Rolls, being somewhat weary of a statesman's life, and desiring to devote himself entirely to his episcopal duties. The Archbishop of Canterbury, Henry Dean, who (as Lord Keeper) held the Great Seal, fell ill in 1502 A.D., and Warham was appointed as his successor in that secular capacity. The archbishop was a comparatively young man, and the new Bishop of London consented, as he thought, to undertake the responsibility temporarily. The archbishop, however, died unexpectedly a few months later, and Warham received from the king the offer of the primacy of All England. Three days before his translation was effected, the title of Lord Keeper was changed to that of Lord Chancellor.

The feast given by the new Archbishop of Canterbury to celebrate his enthronization surpassed in grandeur and magnificence any that had preceded it. When we compare the records with those which describe the frugal entertainment provided by Warham's successor, Dr. Cranmer, we trace in the comparison the splendid conclusion of one era, and the humble commencement of a new epoch, in the history of the Church.

Throughout his career, the hospitality of Warham was conducted on a scale of almost royal magnificence; and, though every luxury was provided for his guests, his own tastes were simple and his habits abstemious. He was a great economist of time; and it is related in his praise that he never played at dice, nor did he, like so many prelates, indulge in field-sports.

Between Warham and King Henry VII. a close friendship existed, and the sovereign was frequently the archbishop's guest at Canterbury.

With the death of the king, in 1509 A.D., the career of Warham as a statesman may be said to have terminated, although he retained the Great Seal until the year 1515 A.D. His action in regard to the marriage of Prince Henry (afterwards Henry VIII.) with the Lady Katharine has been widely misunderstood. Katharine was a daughter of Ferdinand, King of Spain. She had been married to Arthur, Prince of Wales (the eldest son of Henry VII.), but her husband had, it was alleged, died before the marriage was consummated. Warham took up the following position. As lord chancellor he opposed the marriage of Henry with Katharine on the ground that it would tend to cause an international breach between England and Spain. As archbishop he protested against the papal dispensation obtained from the pope, alleging that if the previous marriage had been valid no earthly authority could override the Divine law which

prohibited marriage with a deceased brother's wife;
but if the relations between Prince Arthur and
Katharine had been merely a pre-contract, no papal
dispensation was required. Warham officiated at
the wedding, at which Katharine appeared, not as a
widow, but in the dress and colours which betokened
a virgin bride.

In the year 1510 A.D. the archbishop was appointed by the pope to present the young king,
Henry VIII., with the "golden rose." The rose
was dipped in chrism, perfumed with musk, and
consecrated. The conferring of this gift was a token
of amity on the part of the Roman pontiff, and
amounted to the investiture of a royal personage
with an order of national knighthood by a friendly
sovereign. The presentation to the king took
place with great ceremony in St. Paul's Cathedral.

The relations between Warham and the Archbishop of York, Cardinal Wolsey, who was the
adviser, the friend, and the boon-companion of the
king, have been frequently misrepresented in history.
Wolsey has been credited with having desired to
supplant Warham in the office of chancellor, and
the latter is supposed to have entertained feelings of
petty jealousy and mortification when, in 1515 A.D.,
the Great Seal was transferred to the former. The
real facts of the case are that, as Sir Thomas More
writes in a letter to Erasmus, "The archbishop has
succeeded at last in getting quit of the chancellorship, which he has been labouring to do for some
years;" that during that period Wolsey was unwilling to add to his labours the duties of chancellor, and was anxious that the Archbishop of

Canterbury should retain the office; and that, through the gentleness, amounting almost to weakness, of Warham's character, the personal friendship, if not real affection, between the two men continued unimpaired. Some interesting correspondence, preserved among the documents in the Rolls House, throws considerable light on this point, which has been lost sight of by the majority of historians.

Wolsey had many of the faults, as well as most of the merits, of a powerful, self-reliant, energetic mind. He was overbearing, dictatorial, and impatient of contradiction. The yielding disposition of Warham, and his generous determination to avoid being led into a quarrel with the cardinal, explain why the inevitable disagreements which arose in certain public transactions did not develop into a personal rupture.

Warham, who was at heart a Reformer, attempted the task of rectifying abuses in the ecclesiastical courts, which not only inflicted hardship on many who came for justice, but also brought the whole body of the clergy into contempt and disrepute. The judges in these courts were dependent for their remuneration upon fees, and upon the emoluments of office; and it was a regular custom for the judge to receive money from suitors in his court, not necessarily to purchase a favourable decision, but to ensure an early hearing. Consequently a poor man's case was often delayed for years, because of his inability to pay the honorarium. In February, 1507 A.D., Warham issued from Lambeth his regulations and statutes for the Court of Audience, which were designed to correct these abuses. But the opposition to reform in this respect was too strong. The archbishop, therefore, in order to meet the exceptional condition of affairs, was willing to recede for a time from his high position, and to place the power in the hands of the Archbishop of York as a papal plenipotentiary. The surrender of Warham's authority was only to be temporary, as (although the cardinal subsequently obtained an extension of tenure for his life) it was originally agreed that Wolsey should exercise the legatine power only for seven years.

The opposition to his appointment as legate did not proceed either from the Archbishop of Canterbury or from the king, but from the pope, who was unwilling to invest the powerful minister of the King of England with additional authority; and it is not too much to say that, except for the urgency of Henry VIII. in pressing his views on the unwilling pontiff, Wolsey would never have been made a cardinal. It is important to bear in mind the attitude of the king in this matter, viewed in the light of his subsequent action towards his favourite and towards the English clergy, as well as in reference to the position he took up in later years as to the reformation of the Anglican Church.

Warham, having done his utmost, as we have seen, to correct abuses in the ecclesiastical courts, proceeded to propose certain measures of reform in the Church. For this purpose he summoned the Convocation of Canterbury to meet him at Lambeth, in the year 1518 A.D. To his astonishment he received a most violent and angry letter from Wolsey, who regarded this as an invasion of his rights as legate. An interview took place between the two archbishops. Warham, as usual, gave way; and the result was that a synod was called for the purpose of reforming the Church, although the summonses were not issued in the name of the Archbishop of Canterbury. The meeting was called in Wolsey's name, but was postponed for a year in consequence of the plague which was at the time raging in London. When the synod did at length meet, no business of any importance was transacted.

In 1523 A.D. the Convocations were summoned—that of the northern province being cited to assemble in Westminster, to suit Wolsey's convenience—in order that they might grant a subsidy to the Crown. The Convocation of Canterbury met in the chapter-house of St. Paul's, the writs having been issued by the primate. In the midst of their deliberations a messenger arrived, requiring their attendance before the lord legate. Warham again yielded; but when Wolsey proposed to the amalgamated Convocation that a large sum should be raised for the king, it was humbly represented to him that they could only vote money in their characters as proctors for the clergy, and for that purpose they must return to St. Paul's, and act independently of the Convocation of York. The cardinal at once perceived that he had taken a wrong step, and withdrew.

The rapid fall of Wolsey, when he expressed his inability to further the king's wishes in the matter of the divorce with Queen Katharine, is too well known to be repeated here. But the most astonishing and scandalous act in the drama is found in the fact that King Henry proceeded against his favourite, and, subsequently, against the bishops and clergy who had acquiesced in his appointment as cardinal (solely because they had not dared to oppose the king's wishes), under the Præmunire Statutes.

When Wolsey's overthrow was completed the Great Seal was again offered to Warham, but he declined it on the ground of advancing age and ill health. The chancellorship was thereupon conferred upon Sir Thomas More.

Having ruined Wolsey, Henry VIII. turned his attention to the clergy, and demanded an enormous sum of money as a fine for having acquiesced in the authority conferred on the cardinal by his appointment as papal legate. A controversy between the king and Convocation, extending over several years, resulted in the actual commencement of the Reformation by the reassertion of the royal supremacy, and the submission of the clergy, in 1531 A.D. In 1534 A.D. the Convocation decreed that "the Pope of Rome has no greater jurisdiction conferred on him by God, in Holy Scripture, in this kingdom of England, than any other foreign bishop." Parliament, a few years later, adopted the decision of the Church's representatives.

On August 22, 1532 A.D., the Archbishop of Canterbury, who was over eighty years of age, expired at the residence of his nephew at St. Stephen's, Canterbury.

The character of Warham may to some extent be gleaned from the foregoing sketch of his life. His ability has been underrated because he was dwarfed by the overshadowing of the master-mind of Wolsey.

He was moderate in all his actions; without the skill to originate a great measure, but sagacious enough to see and applaud its wisdom when it was once proposed. Earnestly desirous of reforming abuses, he had neither the energy nor the force of character to carry out his plans in the face of opposition. The self-sacrifice shown in his relations to Wolsey was carried to an extreme, though it was dictated by humbleness rather than cowardice. The following words are the testimony of his friend Erasmus to his good qualities: "What genius! what vivacity! what facility in the most complicated discussions! what erudition! From Warham none ever parted in sorrow. How great is his humility! how edifying his modesty! He alone is ignorant of his eminence; no one is more faithful or more constant in friendship."

ARCHBISHOP CRANMER.
By permission of His Grace the Archbishop of Canterbury.
FROM THE ORIGINAL PICTURE IN LAMBETH PALACE

CHAPTER VII.

THOMAS CRANMER (1533-1556 A.D.).

THOMAS CRANMER was born at Aslacton on July 2, 1484 A.D. His early years were spent at a school where the tyranny and brutality of the master were so great as seriously to impair the memory and intelligence of the scholars, and he appears to have suffered throughout his life from the effects of the treatment he there received. At the age of fourteen he went up to Jesus College, Cambridge, and continued to reside at the university for twenty-five years. Though not deficient in scholarship, **he was** never ranked among the men of learning, and for some years he confined his attention to preparing himself for the legal profession. He was elected a Fellow of his college in 1510 A.D. On his marriage he forfeited his fellowship; but, his wife dying within twelve months, he was reinstated. Turning his attention to the study of theology, he was ordained in 1523 A.D. In 1528 A.D. he went, in his capacity as private tutor, to **the** home of two of his pupils at Waltham, **in** the neighbourhood of which Henry VIII. was residing. Meeting Dr. Gardyner, Secretary of State (afterwards Bishop of Winchester), and Dr. Fox, Lord High Almoner (afterwards Bishop of Hereford), at the house of his pupils' father, Cranmer discussed, and stated his opinion upon, the divorce question which had recently been brought into prominence.

Briefly, the question was as follows:—Queen Katharine had been married to Prince Arthur (eldest son of Henry VII.), who died shortly afterwards. Seven years later the widow became the wife of her husband's brother, on his accession to the throne as Henry VIII. When they had been married nearly twenty years, the king—in consequence, probably, of his attachment to Anne Boleyn—discovered that his conscience pricked him on account of his union with his sister-in-law. It will be remembered that the downfall of Wolsey was occasioned by his non-acquiescence in the king's desire for freedom from his marriage vow. Archbishop Warham had been inclined, though passively, to side with Henry. The suggestion was made that the question should be referred to the pope, with a request for a dispensation to annul the marriage. But the supporters of the queen maintained that the first marriage had never been consummated; that her union with Prince Arthur had, therefore, been merely of the nature of a contract; and that, under these circumstances, there had been no impediment in the way of the marriage with her present husband. On the other hand, it was alleged that, as she had been the wife of the king's brother, it was necessary that the papal sanction for the union should be confirmed. But a further question arose to complicate the controversy. Was the law prohibiting marriage with two brothers in succession a regulation of the Church, or was it a law of God? If the former, the pope's dispensation would hold good, but it could not override the latter.

Cranmer's view, which he expressed in the conversation above referred to, was that if Henry's marriage to Katharine was contrary to the Divine law, it was no marriage at all, and the king was at liberty to wed whom he pleased (provided it were not within the prohibited degrees) without reference to Rome. This point could perfectly well be decided by the ecclesiastical courts of the National Church. If the canonists could prove that marriage with a deceased brother's wife was in opposition to the law of God, and evidence were given that Arthur had been married to Katharine, the king's cause would be gained.

This statement of opinion having been repeated to Henry VIII., Cranmer shortly afterwards received a summons to wait upon his Majesty at Greenwich, and he commanded him to produce a treatise in which his argument was to be supported by the authority of Holy Scripture, of the general councils, and of the Fathers. He accepted the hospitality of Anne Boleyn's father, the Earl of Wiltshire, at Durham Place, overlooking the Thames, where he had the use of the magnificent library belonging to his host; and was appointed one of the royal chaplains.

After Cranmer's treatise had received the royal imprimatur, it was laid before the two Universities and the House of Commons. The author was next selected as advocate for the king on an embassy to the papal court. Although the pope postponed indefinitely a public discussion of the divorce question, he treated Cranmer with every mark of respect, and made him "Penitentiary of England," *i.e.* the officer on whom was conferred the power of granting all papal dispensations. He remained abroad for some time, but returned to England in the spring of 1531 A.D. In the following year, being again in Germany, he married, as his second wife, the niece of his friend, the Reformer Osiander. This fact goes far to corroborate Cranmer's own statement, that he never sought, desired, nor expected the primacy of the Church of England.

At Warham's death, however, the king nominated Cranmer to the archbishopric, feeling that he was the man of all others who could render the most effective assistance in obtaining the divorce. The *congé d'élire* was issued; the chapter proceeded to the election; all the legal forms were prepared; and on March 30, 1533 A.D., Thomas Cranmer was consecrated at Westminster. The appointment was very unpopular. The new archbishop had done nothing to justify his extraordinary rise; and the reason of his nomination to the see was well known, and proportionately resented, by those who felt indignant at the insult offered to the highest lady in the land. A writ is extant, issued by Henry in 1534 A.D., calling upon the dukes, viscounts, barons, etc., to protect the Lord Archbishop of Canterbury during the visitation of his clergy. This shows the strong feeling there was against him.

Crumwell, the king's favourite minister, had, in the mean time, obtained an Act of Parliament (which was designed to prevent the possibility of the final decision on the divorce question being further delayed by an appeal to Rome) rendering more stringent certain acts which had been passed in previous reigns. It was there enacted that no appeals should be made outside the realm, but that the courts spiritual and temporal within the king's dominion should try, and decide, all causes testamentary, matrimonial, relating to tithes, oblations, obventions, and the like.

It is interesting to notice how the determination, which had for many years been growing among clergy and laity alike, to restrict the aggressions and usurped authority of the papal see in England, received such powerful aid through the king's quarrel with Rome on a personal question. It is probable that the final rupture with the papacy, which the Reformation effected, would have been longer delayed (although it certainly would not have been averted) had it not been for the support which the powerful alliance of Henry, in serving his own ends, gave to the movement.

The first public act of the new archbishop was that of presiding at the session of Convocation, which, after long and vehement debates on the various points submitted by the king, decided, by a majority of 253 to 19, that marriage with a deceased brother's wife was contrary to the law of God.

In order that all the proceedings in connection with the divorce might present an appearance of justice and legality, Cranmer (probably at the royal instigation) wrote a letter to Henry, "praying the king's licence to put an end to all doubts with respect to the validity of the marriage with Katharine, by permitting him to hear and determine the cause of the divorce in his archiepiscopal court." To this request his Majesty graciously assented, cheerfully submitting to be judged by the primate, notwithstanding the tenacity with which he had always held to the royal claim to supremacy in all causes and over all persons, both ecclesiastical and civil.

The judgment was delivered on May 23, 1533 A.D., in which it was decreed that the marriage with Queen Katharine was null and void. Cranmer, in his anxiety to meet the wishes of his royal master, gave little thought to the faithful and devoted wife who was thus degraded and insulted by a travesty of justice; and the vehemence of the feeling which grew up throughout the country for a time placed the archbishop's very life in danger. To add to his unhappiness, the king, having obtained from the primate the service he required, treated him with studied neglect.

One great step towards the reformation of the Church of England was taken when the royal supremacy was definitely established. It then only remained for the king and the primate to devise legislation which would meet the various difficulties as they arose. They did not seek to eradicate the Catholic religion; on the contrary, each maintained his adherence to Catholicism, and desired to advance it. But both wished to separate it from Romanism.

The sentence of excommunication pronounced by the Bishop of Rome upon the King of England, in consequence of the repudiation of papal authority, roused the nation, and excited a storm of indignation. It was met by the decision of Convocation, which was soon followed by that of Parliament, that "the Bishop of Rome has no greater jurisdiction given him in this Realm of England than any other foreign bishop;" and thus the Church of England was, by a synodical act, separated from the see of Rome, and released from the usurped dominion which she had never synodically recognised, and against which she had bravely struggled for several centuries.

The circumstances connected with the trial of Anne Boleyn, and the reasons for Cranmer's action in the matter, are almost impossible to arrive at, owing to the meagreness of the records. There is, however, little doubt that the archbishop was kept without clear and official information of the real charges against the queen, and of the result of the court of inquiry. At the same time, we can hardly acquit him of a want of impartiality, in the easy compliance with the wishes of the king which he displayed, when he practically consented to condemn the unhappy wife of his royal master before proof of her guilt was adduced.

The whole circumstances are so shrouded in mystery that it will probably never be known whether she was guilty or innocent of the charges made against her. At the same time, the archbishop must have realized that if the marriage had "always been without effect," as he adjudged it to have been, then Anne Boleyn could not with justice be condemned to death for unfaithfulness (assuming the truth of the accusations) to a man who had never been her lawful husband. Convocation showed the same pliability as the primate; and the decision was subscribed by both houses. The unfortunate queen was beheaded.

For several years, commencing in 1535 A.D., the spoliation of the monasteries and religious houses progressed, to the satisfaction of the king, under his minister, Thomas Crumwell. With the exception of the creation of six new sees, poorly endowed, and the establishment of Trinity College, Cambridge, almost the whole of the confiscated wealth was squandered in bribes, or went to enrich the coffers of the monarch. The restoration of a secular chapter at Canterbury, where the regulars of Christ Church had held sway since the Conquest, was preceded by the ridiculous exhibition of hostility against the memory of Thomas à Becket. The canonized primate was cited by the Attorney-General to answer to a charge of treason, contumacy, and rebellion, the summons being read at the shrine by a pursuivant for thirty consecutive days. As the saint showed no inclination to appear before his judges, the shrine was demolished, and the priceless treasures belonging to it were appropriated to the king.

In 1539 A.D., after an unsuccessful conference with an embassy representing the foreign Protestants, who proposed that the Church of England should accept as its doctrinal formulary the Confession of Augsburg, the king promoted the passing through Parliament of the Statute of the Six Articles, the effect of which was temporarily to restore the doctrine of transubstantiation, the celibacy of the clergy, private masses, communion in one kind, and compulsory confession. The importance of this Act consists, not so much in its provisions (which were modified in 1543 A.D., and repealed in 1547 A.D.), as in the demonstration it affords of the state of the religious opinions of Henry VIII. and of Cranmer at that time. Though they were both willing to examine any proposal suggested by those who had come under the influence of the German Protestants, they were in no hurry, having secured the repudiation of papal supremacy, to overthrow doctrines and ceremonies in the Church, unless they were well assured that something better could be substituted. The measure, though not strictly enforced, rendered it necessary for Cranmer to send his wife back to Germany, lest he might be proceeded against, for we have abundant evidence to show that the archbishop had at this time many bitter enemies. The failure of the conspiracy against him, through the personal support and protection of the king (which is so graphically described by Shakespeare), is too well known to need repetition.

The domestic life of the primate was simple and regular. He rose at five o'clock, and occupied the first hours of the day in devotion and reading. At nine he received visitors, and transacted business till dinner at one. Later he received any suitor or petitioner who claimed his attention, after which he indulged in field-sports (if in the country) or in a game of chess until five, when he repaired to the chapel. Supper, and the society of his guests, filled up the evening until nine, when he retired to rest.

The position taken up by Cranmer in regard to the English version of the Bible was such as to secure for him the gratitude of posterity. John

Rogers, writing under the pseudonym of Matthew, had lately published a Bible in English, based on the translations of Tyndale and Coverdale. The archbishop approved of this version, and the royal injunctions of 1538 A.D. ordered that a copy should be set up in a convenient place in every parish church. The unwillingness of the king to allow Convocation to deal with and put forward an authorised translation of the Scriptures induced the primate to place the work in the hands of a committee of learned divines from the two universities, and subsequently Cranmer's, or the "Great Bible," came into general use. This was to some extent superseded in the following reigns; and, in spite of every effort on the part of the ecclesiastical authorities, the Church of England possessed no universally accepted version of the Scriptures until the reign of James I., when that translation appeared which is still in use.

Cranmer was the leading spirit in the translation of the service-books into the vernacular. We are indebted to him for the first English Litany, issued in 1543 A.D., which, with very slight alterations, is practically that which we now use. He also took part in the production of "The Institution of a Christian Man," afterwards called "The Bishop's Book"—a volume of instruction for the laity—with which were incorporated the "Ten Articles," drawn up by Convocation in 1536 A.D., and intended to formulate the position of the Church of England on certain doctrinal and ceremonial points. He was the author of several of the "Homilies" the collection of which was brought out under his direction shortly after the accession of Edward VI.

The archbishop was the head of the revising committee, by whom the First Prayer-book of Edward VI. was issued in 1549 A.D. This, the first complete version in English of the service-books of the Church, gives clear evidence of the Catholic spirit by which the primate was prompted. As we have seen, he repudiated the supremacy of the Bishop of Rome, but he had no desire to yield to the influence of the Protestant party by sweeping away those beliefs and practices which had come down to the Anglican Church from primitive times. The Second Prayer-book of Edward VI., put forward in 1552 A.D. shortly before the king's death, was also due, in some degree, to Cranmer, whose sacramental views appear to have undergone considerable alteration in the space of a few years. He changed from transubstantiation to the Lutheran doctrine of consubstantiation, and in 1550 A.D. he adopted the view of the Eucharist, which he set forth at length in his "Defence of the True and Catholic Doctrine of the Sacrament," wherein he asserts that there is a real *spiritual* presence conveyed to the believer, but discards many of the dogmas which mediæval theology had built upon this premise.

The accession of Mary to the throne, on the death of her half-brother, was the commencement of a veritable reign of terror. The archbishop soon felt the weight of the royal displeasure. The queen had never forgotten or forgiven the part he had taken in the divorce proceedings against her mother, Queen Katharine. In 1555 A.D., Cranmer, together with Ridley and Latimer, was tried at Oxford before a committee of priests, and the three divines were condemned for being guilty of heresy. A year and a half later the imprisoned primate was cited to appear at Rome before the pope within eighty days, and was shortly afterwards brought for trial before Dr. Brooks, Bishop of Gloucester, as the pope's representative. He denied the jurisdiction of a court presided over by a papal commissioner, and was remanded. In December, 1555 A.D., the Bishop of Rome issued sentence, condemning him for having brought in "the heresy of Berengarius, and the false and heretical doctrines of Luther," and appointing two bishops to degrade him from the archiepiscopal rank. In an unhappy moment of weakness the primate was induced to admit the authority of the pope in a paper commonly called his first recantation. Under the promise of restoration to liberty, he signed paper after paper, repudiating his views on the Holy Eucharist, and denouncing the Protestant system. At length, when he realized that the queen had throughout intended to sacrifice him, he boldly announced his allegiance to the form of faith for which he had been condemned, and was burnt at the stake on March 21, 1556 A.D.

The character of Cranmer is best judged from the facts of his life. His weakness and lack of courage it is impossible to deny; yet few men could have passed unscathed through the trials which fell to his lot. The Church of England owes him an unceasing debt of gratitude for his scriptural and liturgical labours, of which we enjoy the fruit even to this day.

ARCHBISHOP PARKER.
By permission of His Grace the Archbishop of Canterbury.
FROM AN OLD PORTRAIT IN LAMBETH PALACE.

CHAPTER VIII.

MATTHEW PARKER (1559-1575 A.D.).

MATTHEW PARKER was the son of William Parker a tradesman, and was born at Norwich on August 6, 1504 A.D. His father died when he was only twelve years of age; but his mother, who had in the mean time married again, sent him in due course to Corpus Christi College, Cambridge, where he took his degree in 1525 A.D., being ordained deacon and priest two years later. He was early distinguished as a scholar, and was elected to a fellowship of his college in 1528 A.D. He was appointed Master of Corpus, under royal mandate, in 1544 A.D., and shortly afterwards became Vice-Chancellor of the University.

Parker had been in orders for several years when he first received a licence to preach, but it was not long before he attracted attention by the ability and eloquence of his sermons. In 1535 A.D. he was made chaplain to Anne Boleyn, for whom he entertained an affectionate regard, and by whom he was entreated, only a few days before her death, to watch over the interests of her daughter, afterwards Queen Elizabeth. He subsequently became chaplain to the king (Henry VIII.). For thirteen years he lived at Stoke-by-Clare, the deanery of which he held by virtue of his office as queen's chaplain. The threatened dissolution of the deanery and confiscation of its revenues were averted during the lifetime of Henry VIII. through the intercession of the Queen Consort, Katharine Parr, but were carried out under the Protectorate in 1547 A.D., when Parker was presented to the deanery of Lincoln. In June of the same year, notwithstanding that the Act which authorised the marriage of the clergy had not yet been passed, he married Margaret Harleston, to whom he had been engaged for seven years. A woman of refinement and culture, Mrs. Parker proved to be an admirable wife, managing his household affairs with economy, while sharing her husband's spirit of hospitality and generosity.

For a long period Parker resolutely declined the repeated invitations which were addressed to him, either directly or indirectly, by members of the Government, to take part in public affairs. His conduct in addressing the insurgents under Kett, and endeavouring to quell the insurrection, led to a renewal of these requests, which, however, were powerless to alter his decision.

When Queen Mary ascended the throne, Parker was deprived of all his preferments, and lived a life of retirement, happy in the domestic peace and literary leisure he enjoyed, with no drawback save the uncertainty and anxiety lest at any moment he might be accused of heresy before the ecclesiastical judge by some informer desiring to curry favour at court.

With the accession of Elizabeth his difficulties were by no means at an end, as the queen was obstinately opposed to the marriage of the clergy, while Parker was equally determined not to be separated from his wife and family, the latter consisting of two sons, two children having died in infancy.

The religious parties in England at this time were numerous and divided. The prevalent idea in these days that all Catholics were Romanists, and all those who were not Romanists were Protestants, is entirely erroneous and misleading. In Parker's time, the Protestants were the reformed Church of England, *i.e.* those who "protested" against the usurpations of Rome, or, in other words, the Anglo-Catholics. Opposed to the English reformers stood the Puritans, the representatives of Calvinism. During the reign of Elizabeth we find the establishment of the Romish sect without any hierarchy (which was only introduced during the present century), who represented, not the primitive Church, but the then existing Roman government. On the Continent, at this period, were various bodies of reformers—Lutherans, Zwinglians, Calvinists, etc.—between whom and the leaders of the Reformation in England there was no real sympathy; the latter desiring to retain their ecclesiastical system, after purging it from the additions of mediæval superstition, while the former wished to sweep away the ancient fabric, and build a new sect upon its ruins. At the same time, the Puritan influence from abroad left its impress upon the tone and character of the second Prayer-book of Edward VI., that of 1552 A.D.

It must be remembered that the Reformation was a movement from within the Church, and had been growing for nearly two centuries. The assertion made by some writers that the clergy generally were papists at heart, and joined the Reformation with great reluctance, is entirely without proof, and is opposed to all the facts of which we are cognisant. Out of a body of nearly 10,000 clergy, the number of those who were deprived under Queen Elizabeth for refusing to take the oath of supremacy, or for demurring to the English " offices," amounted only to 189, of whom no less than fourteen were bishops, these being almost entirely representatives of the " old learning." Thus the supporters of the statement that the Reformation was forced upon an unwilling Romanist clergy must either acknowledge themselves mistaken, or confess that those whom they uphold and admire were almost all hypocrites and cowards. The true historical view is that for a long period there had been a growing uneasiness throughout the country at the way in which successive kings had, for their own personal interests, played into the hands of the popes, and an increasing desire to be free from the accretions of Romanist dogmas, which had almost insensibly been superimposed upon the doctrinal and ceremonial position of the Anglican Church. The quarrel between the autocratic king, Henry VIII., and the papal see furnished exactly the opportunity for which the Church and nation had been waiting, and the quiet and peaceful manner in which the alteration was effected, under the favourable conditions of Elizabeth's reign, proves conclusively that the change in the religious character of the people was deep-seated and genuine.

Queen Elizabeth succeeded to the throne in November, 1558 A.D. Like her father and Cranmer she was a Catholic at heart, though she was as firmly determined as they were to resist the pretensions of Rome. One of her first public acts was to open negotiations with the pope. Had the aged and almost imbecile Paul IV. been able to free himself from the unwise counsels of the French ambassador, the future relations of the Anglican Church to Romanism might have been very different from what they became. But when his insolent reply was returned to the overtures of the queen, the final rupture became inevitable; and from that time Elizabeth and her advisers were compelled to make considerable concessions to the foreign Protestants (the majority of whom were Calvinists), in order to secure their support against Rome.

Great difficulty was experienced by Cecil, the queen's favourite and confidential minister, in inducing Parker to emerge from his retirement and take his position in public affairs. His ill health, combined with his self-depreciation, made him most unwilling to come forward. He was, however, persuaded to act on the Royal Commission appointed to consider the question of ecclesiastical reform. The queen and Cecil, and probably Parker himself, desired the restoration, with slight modifications, of the first Prayer-book of Edward VI. But, probably in deference to the advice of the latter, who saw that it was better to sacrifice something than to lose everything, the second Prayer-book was adopted as the basis of revision.

The first business of Parliament was to substitute,

at Elizabeth's initiative, the title of "supreme governor" for that of "Head of the Church," which her father had adopted. The Act of Supremacy encountered fierce opposition at the hands of the extreme papists and extreme puritans before it became law. The Spoliation Bills (the one attaching the firstfruits and tenths of ecclesiastical benefices to the Crown, and the other empowering the sovereign, on the avoidance of a see, to annex any of its landed property, giving in exchange certain impropriate tithes) were strenuously combated by the bishops, and only passed through the Commons by a narrow majority. The Act of Uniformity, authorising the revised Prayer-book, was passed a few months later. Less than one hundred of the clergy refused to conform to its provisions.

Cardinal Pole, who succeeded Cranmer as Archbishop of Canterbury, died within twenty-four hours of Queen Mary. The necessity for establishing the sovereignty of Queen Elizabeth, and for taking measures to preserve the continuity of the primacy, was the cause of the delay in appointing a successor to the archbishopric. Parker's retiring disposition led him to decline the appointment when it was first offered to him, but he subsequently acquiesced, the *congé d'élire* was issued on May 18, and the election was held on August 1. The consecration of Parker took place in the Chapel of Lambeth Palace on December 17, 1559 A.D. It was conducted strictly in accordance with the second ordinal of Edward VI. The bishops who took part in his consecration were William Barlow, formerly Bishop of Bath and Wells, and now Bishop-elect of

Chichester, who presided, and performed that portion of the ceremonial which, under ordinary circumstances, would have devolved upon the metropolitan; John Hodgkins, who had been consecrated in St. Paul's Cathedral by the Bishop of London under the old form, in accordance with the rites of the Sarum pontifical, as Suffragan Bishop of Bedford; Miles Coverdale, who had been consecrated Bishop of Exeter in 1551 A.D. by Cranmer; and John Scory, late Bishop of Rochester, and now Bishop-elect of Hereford. Barlow, Hodgkins, and Scory appeared in their episcopal vestments, Coverdale in a cassock, and the archbishop-elect in his scarlet robes, such as are now worn in Convocation. The sermon was preached by Scory; and Bishop Barlow, when celebrating, was vested in a silk cope. Every detail of the consecration is preserved in Parker's register, written by himself; the Mandate for the consecration is preserved in the Record office; and thus we have a contemporary and anticipatory refutation of the falsehoods many years afterwards invented and propagated by certain unprincipled Romanists in the "Nag's Head Fable," which has been acknowledged to have been an absolutely untrue fiction by such learned and eminent Romanist writers as Charles Butler, Canon Tierney, and, above all, Dr. Lingard.

The difference between the Churches of England and Rome was accentuated by the non-recognition of Elizabeth as a Catholic sovereign in the issue of invitations to the Council of Trent, and the refusal of the queen to allow the papal nuncio to land on her shores. The Anglican Church, continued to be what she always had been, the Catholic Church of this realm, although she had now definitely and finally broken away from the influence of, and purged herself from the errors she had learnt through her alliance with the Roman Church.

Four days after his own consecration, Archbishop Parker consecrated four new bishops in Lambeth Chapel; on January 21, 1560 A.D., five bishops; and four more in March, to fill the unprecedented number of vacancies in the episcopal sees. The plague which proved so fatal to the bishops at the close of Mary's reign had also thinned the ranks of the clergy to such an extent that many of the diocesans ordained men who exhibited the enthusiasm of piety without reference to their learning or other qualifications. The archbishop deprecated this course, and adopted the wiser plan of supplementing the clerical force by a contingent of lay helpers.

In 1562 A.D. the celebrated "Apology" of Bishop Jewel appeared, and was soon translated into almost all the languages of Europe. In Mary's reign, Jewel had, under intimidation, renounced all that laid him open to a suspicion of Protestantism; but soon after, repenting and recanting, he fled abroad. Having been appointed to preach at Paul's Cross in June, 1559 A.D., he took very high ground, maintaining the Catholicism of the Church of England, and declaring that where the Church of Rome differed from the Church of England, the former was mediæval, the latter primitive. Being thus brought under the notice of Archbishop Parker, he was elected to the see of Salisbury, and consecrated in 1560 A.D. His "Apology" was a brave and comprehensive defence of the position of the Anglican Church, and still ranks among the classical literature of Anglicanism.

One of Parker's great works was to bring out, with the co-operation of a body of translators, a new version of the Scriptures called "The Bishops' Bible," which was, however, opposed by the Puritans, and was not "authorised" till 1604 A.D., a few years before the issue of our existing "Authorised Version."

The archbishop was also very fully occupied at this time in the preparation of the Articles. The "Thirteen Articles," setting forth the reforming opinions of the Lutheran divines, which were published in 1538 A.D., were never formally accepted, but were taken as a basis of revision by Cranmer, who produced "Forty-two Articles." These were approved by Convocation, and received the royal authority in 1553 A.D.; but, on Mary's accession two months later, they were suppressed. In 1563 A.D., under Parker's direction, Thirty-eight Articles were issued, with the approval of Convocation only. These were again revised in 1571 A.D., when they assumed their present order and number. They were accepted by Convocation, sanctioned by Parliament, and ratified by Queen Elizabeth, and have ever since been regarded as the test of orthodox Churchmanship.

The strong Puritan faction, which gave evidence of its vitality in the Convocation of 1563 A.D., received considerable support from the championship of the Earl of Leicester, an unscrupulous profligate, whom the queen regarded with such feelings of affection as gave him a powerful influence over her. The Puritans deliberately conducted Divine service with slovenly irreverence. Some would not even kneel at the Holy Communion, others would not wear a surplice. Elizabeth was roused to anger, and ordered the archbishop to confer with his suffragans, and to take such measures as were requisite to establish a reverent uniformity. But she would give him no support or assistance, fearing lest she should thereby offend Leicester, and incense the party who looked up to him; and consequently she shifted the whole onus and responsibility on to the shoulders of the primate and the bishops.

Parker, in consequence, decided that his powers were sufficient by themselves to warrant the issue of a code of rules which would secure " decency, distinction, and order for the time." A book of " Advertisements " was accordingly drawn up, containing articles ranged under four heads; for doctrine and preaching; for administration of prayer and sacraments; for certain orders in ecclesiastical policy; and for outward apparel of persons ecclesiastical. They were compiled in 1564 A.D., published early in the following year, but not generally circulated until March, 1566 A.D. They were quoted as authoritative in the Canons of 1571 A.D., although it is doubtful if they ever received the queen's sanction; but they were afterwards ratified by Charles I.

In April, 1570 A.D., a Bull was signed by Pope Pius V., excommunicating Elizabeth, denouncing her as a usurper, and commanding her subjects to violate their oaths of allegiance. This was found posted on the gates of London House. The advanced Catholics in the ranks of the clergy seem to have remained faithful to the throne at this crisis, and the queen's confidence in their loyalty was expressed in the manifesto she issued at the time. The Commons, however, desired to subject all priests to the test of declaring their assent to the Thirty-nine Articles. The Act requiring this was passed in spite of the disapproval of Elizabeth, although she ultimately gave way and granted her royal consent.

The Romish schism in England dates from the same year, its adherents being governed by priests with special commissions from the pope, and then by bishops *in partibus*. The practice of giving English titles to the intruding Roman episcopate dates from the year 1850 A.D.

The first Puritan schism took place in 1573 A.D. In a few years several subdivisions among the sect occurred, such as the "Precisians" and the "Brownists," the latter called after Robert Brown, who subsequently founded the Independents or Congregationalists.

In addition to his literary labours in connection with the translation of the Bible, the revision of the Liturgy, and the preparation of the Articles and Homilies, Parker was the writer or editor of a very large number of important works. His history, "De Antiquitate Britannicæ Ecclesiæ," published in 1572 A.D., displays an extraordinary amount of research. It is marvellous how the archbishop, with the unceasing pressure of his duties as primate, during one of the most critical epochs of the Church's history, was able to find the leisure for an amount of literary work which would have done credit to one whose whole time was devoted to study and writing.

Parker's death took place on May 17, 1575 A.D., his beloved and faithful wife having pre-deceased him by five years. He was buried in the Chapel of Lambeth Palace, in a tomb which he had prepared during his lifetime. The Puritans, who hated him when living, pursued him with their malignity even after his death. In the troublous times of Charles I. his body was dug up and thrown on to a dunghill, the lead of the coffin being sold. After the restoration of Charles II., Sir William Dugdale, hearing of the circumstances, mentioned the matter to Archbishop Sancroft. A careful search was made, and the bones were recovered and decently interred in the body of the chapel, just below the sanctuary steps. The following suggestive inscription can still be seen: "Corpus Matthæi Archiepiscopi tandem hic quiescit."

In the death of Archbishop Parker the Church of England lost the leader who had so wisely guided her course through a period of storm and perplexity, and whose claims on the gratitude of posterity are enhanced by the fact that during his lifetime he received little save hostility and indifference. Archdeacon Hardwicke sums up the archbishop's character and work when he says that "almost entirely by his skill the vessel he was called upon to pilot was saved from breaking on the rock of mediæval superstitions, or else from drifting away into the whirlpool of licentiousness and unbelief."

ARCHBISHOP LAUD.
By permission of His Grace the Archbishop of Canterbury.
FROM THE ORIGINAL PICTURE, BY VANDYCK, IN LAMBETH PALACE.

CHAPTER IX.

WILLIAM LAUD (1633-1645 A.D.).

THE career of Edmund Grindal, who had been successively Bishop of London and Archbishop of York, and succeeded Parker as Archbishop of Canterbury in 1576 A.D., does not call for any special mention. He revived the Puritan practice of "prophesyings," which had been suppressed by his predecessor, and was, in consequence of his refusal to obey the queen's order that they should be discontinued, confined to his house and suspended for six months. In 1582 A.D. he tendered a qualified submission, and died in the following year.

John Whitgift, Bishop of Worcester, was next chosen by Elizabeth as primate, and the appointment was a judicious one, as he proved himself a wise and firm disciplinarian at a time when the turbulence of the ultra-Protestants required to be checked with vigour. Finding that many of the clergy were dissenters at heart, he drew up a series of canons, embodying the three tests which had been enforced by royal authority in 1583 A.D. The three tests were that all in Holy Orders should acknowledge the Prayer-book, the Articles, and the royal supremacy. This aroused a storm of indignation from the Puritans, who proceeded to alienate sympathy from themselves by publishing scurrilous libels on the bishops. A strong Act was passed in 1593 A.D., emanating from the Commons, for enforcing discipline.

The closing years of Elizabeth's reign were marked by the growing popularity of the Church, which was maintained under James I. in spite of the Presbyterian views with which he was credited. The most important result of the Hampton Court Conference of 1604 A.D., over which the king presided, was that it led to a revision of the Bible, which was brought out in 1611 A.D., and soon, from its superiority to other versions, gained universal acceptance, and still exists as our "authorised" version, although it was never "authorised" either by Convocation, or by Parliament, or by the king in Council. To Whitgift, who died shortly after the conference, "the Church of England owes, under God, the preservation of its order and discipline, and the rescue of its property from the covetous grasp of the queen and courtiers."

Bancroft's policy, though successful in driving nonconformity into concealment, was injudicious, inasmuch as it alienated many from Anglicanism by reason of its interference with the liberty of the subject. In 1610 A.D. Episcopacy was restored in Scotland.

Abbot, a bigoted man of Calvinistic principles, succeeded Bancroft in the same year. He lost favour at Court before the death of James I.; and for some years after the accession of Charles I. he was practically no longer primate, the king himself having placed Laud at the head of ecclesiastical affairs from the commencement of his reign.

William Laud was born at Reading on October 7, 1573 A.D., and at the age of sixteen went up to St. John's College, Oxford. He became Fellow of his college in 1593 A.D., and was ordained in 1600 A.D. In 1611 A.D. he was elected President of St. John's, in spite of the strenuous opposition of Archbishop Abbot, and the same year he was appointed by the king to be one of his chaplains. Four years later he was presented to the deanery of Gloucester, where, notwithstanding the fierce and even turbulent resistance of the Puritans, he was enabled to repair the fabric of the cathedral, and introduce decency and order into the conduct of the services. The Bishop of Gloucester at that time was an inflexible Calvinist, and refused ever again to enter the cathedral in consequence of these reforms.

Laud was consecrated as Bishop of St. David's in 1621 A.D., but he was unable for some time to attend to his episcopal duties in his remote diocese, his presence being almost continually required at Court, where his abilities had been recognised by the king. His character as a divine was established through the controversy he held with the Jesuit, John Percy, whose historical name is Fisher; and his judgment and statesmanship were appreciated by Buckingham, whose esteem and friendship he retained in spite of the successful opposition he showed towards the proposed misappropriation of the funds of the Charterhouse, which the minister had proposed with a view to replenishing the royal treasury.

The death of King James, which occurred in 1625 A.D., precipitated a political reformation, the tendency of the times being opposed to the absolutest theory of government. The accession of Charles I., a man of amiable disposition and virtuous life, but utterly devoid of the ability of the statesman, was powerless to prevent the rebellion, in which the principles of the Church were proscribed, her clergy persecuted with fearful severity, and her temples wrecked by spiteful and triumphant fanatics.

The marriage of the young king to Henrietta Maria, daughter of the King of France, an uncompromising Romanist, was most unfortunate for the country, which was in no mood to grant concessions to or encourage those who favoured the papacy. Charles himself was a pronounced and consistent Churchman, and zealous in the interests of Anglicanism, but was unable to tolerate any form of dissent, and least of all the Calvinistic school, now popular among the English laity. This disposition naturally laid him open to the suspicion of a leaning towards Rome, and gave force to the Puritan dissatisfaction which culminated in the cry of "No Arminianism!" which was as popular as the cry of "No popery!"

One of the first matters which engaged the attention of the new Parliament was an attack on Dr. Montague, Rector of Stamford Rivers, for having, in a book he wrote controverting the statements of certain Jesuits, described the Roman Church as a branch of the true Church, although a corrupt branch. When the king asked the Commons to vote supplies to carry on the war against Spain, on which the Duke of Buckingham had rashly entered, they only granted an insignificant sum, and reverted to the case of Montague. Charles thereupon angrily dissolved that Parliament and called another together the following year, but with no better success, for it impeached the Duke of Buckingham, to save whom the king at once dissolved this second Parliament, and had recourse to forced loans in order to raise money for his expeditions.

In 1626 A.D. Andrewes, the great and saintly Bishop of Winchester, died. Laud succeeded him in the office of Dean of the Chapel Royal, which brought him into still closer relations with the king.

The third Parliament of Charles was called together in 1628 A.D., in order that the king might obtain funds for prosecuting the war with France, in which the English troops had hitherto been worsted. Before the Commons would vote the necessary subsidies they drew up the Petition of Right, which placed an effectual check on the absolutism of the monarch, and the king was compelled by necessity to assent to its provisions. The legislature next drew up the "Remonstrance" against the "Arminian" clergy—directed specially against Bishop Neile of Winchester, and Bishop Laud—at which Charles showed his resentment by proroguing Parliament and promoting Laud from the see of Bath and Wells to that of London, and appointing Dr. Montague to be Bishop of Chichester. At this time Laud suffered an irreparable loss in the death, by the hand of an assassin, of his friend the Duke of Buckingham, whose place he took as the adviser, counsellor, and intimate friend of the king.

Among the many and varied reforms effected by Laud was that of the University of Oxford, by the framing of the new statutes, and in other ways. His labours and zeal were recognised by his being elected, in 1630 A.D., as Chancellor of the University.

In his new diocese of London Laud detected the rapid growth of Calvinism, and on his advice the king caused the Thirty-nine Articles to be republished, with a royal declaration (drawn up by the Bishop of London) prefixed to them, affirming that Convocation is the proper body to order and settle ecclesiastial affairs; that only the plain, literal and grammatical sense should be put upon the Articles; and that all disputation respecting them should cease.

The Puritans bitterly opposed the declaration, and in deference to the views of the extreme party, the Commons voted the "Vow," in which they "claimed, protested, and avowed for truth" the Calvinistic sense of the Articles, adding that "we reject the sense of the Jesuits and Arminians, and all others, wherein they differ from us." This third Parliament was, in 1629 A.D., dissolved by the king, who governed without the advice of the legislature for eleven years.

The most unpopular, and perhaps the most reprehensible, part of Charles's system was the active employment of the High Commission and Star Chamber Courts. The former had been established in 1559 A.D., the latter as early as 1487 A.D. The barbarous treatment of the libellers sentenced in these courts, however gross the offence of the prisoner, cannot be defended. It can only be explained as part of the system of absolutism, in ecclesiastical as well as civil matters, which the king exercised so unwisely and unconstitutionally that it led to the revolution, and to his own violent death. But the position of Laud in the matter has been so grossly misrepresented, that it is necessary to point out that his influence in the Star Chamber was simply that of the one spiritual lord in a council of seven members, and we have no evidence to show that he ever exerted his influence in the direction of severity.

On the other hand, for those proceedings in Church affairs which the Puritans stigmatized as "innovations" in religion, Laud may be considered almost exclusively responsible. He endeavoured to enforce the law, in regard to doctrine and ritual, as it stood, and in the difficulties of his task he undoubtedly made use of the royal assumption of prerogative which, if it had been allowed to grow, would infallibly have endangered the religious liberty of the nation. Laud, however, had to protect the Church from dangerous and unscrupulous foes, who were bent on the destruction of its Catholicity, and on metamorphosing it into a Calvinistic sect.

In 1633 A.D., on the death of Archbishop Abbot, Laud was appointed to the primacy. For some years the direction of Church affairs had been practically in his hands; first, during the period of Abbot's suspension, when Laud was at the head of the commission formed to discharge the functions of the office; and later, when the archbishop's age and infirmities almost entirely incapacitated him from active work of any kind, and his duties to a large extent devolved upon the Bishop of London.

The position of the Lord Primate was at that time a very high one, and was enhanced by the important secular positions which he held. English nobles and foreign ambassadors paid their court to him at Lambeth. He did not look for happiness in his new life—indeed, he seems from the first to have regarded it with apprehension. In a letter to Strafford he surmises that his health would suffer from want of exercise, as he would now slide over in a barge from Lambeth to Court instead of jolting over the stones from London House to Whitehall. We have few glimpses of his domestic life, but amongst other pets he seems to have owned a tortoise. The shell of this tortoise has been preserved in the Muniment-room at Lambeth Palace, bearing an inscription which tells that it belonged to Archbishop Laud, that it lived for a hundred and twenty years, and that it was at last "mortally killed" by a gardener.

One of Laud's first acts, after succeeding to the archbishopric of Canterbury, was to hold a metropolitical visitation of all the dioceses in the province. His efforts to protect the Holy Tables from desecration were violently opposed in many places. An innovation had recently been made by which they had been moved into the body of the church, and the result was that they were frequently used as a receptacle for cloaks and hats, or as suitable places for transacting the churchwardens' accounts. Laud ordered that the Holy Tables should be replaced altar-wise against the east walls, and fenced off by a railing from the body of the chancel. The bishops, with the exception of Bishop Williams of Lincoln, loyally supported him in the matter, and gradually decency and order were restored in the churches.

Laud then proceeded to make considerable efforts to ameliorate the condition of the London clergy. The poverty of a considerable number of them was deplorable. With the assistance of Juxon, who succeeded him as Bishop of London in 1633 A.D., Laud was enabled to effect a vast improvement, which would have been carried further had not the troubles of the time increased upon him.

The archbishop's attention was now called to the state of Ireland, the history of which, during his primacy, was so closely associated with the memory of his friend Strafford. However severely we may be inclined to criticize the injudicious, and sometimes even the tyrannical exercise of his authority, it cannot be denied that, under Strafford, Ireland, which till then had been only a trouble and expense to the Crown, became a source of riches and strength. There was much in common between the two men in their administration. Both were actuated by a desire to promote the public good; both were careful, however harshly they acted, to keep within the limits of the existing powers of government; both were careless of popularity. Neither of them ever wavered for a moment in his determination to do what he felt to be just and right, although they were not, perhaps, always inclined to allow mercy to influence their policy.

In Scotland, whither Laud had accompanied

King James in 1620 A.D., and Charles in 1633 A.D., no attention was paid to Catholic antiquity or to uniformity in worship. The archbishop decided if possible to introduce the English liturgy, but was overruled, and a Scotch Service-book was drawn up, with the approval of the Scotch divines, containing a certain number of variations from our Anglican Prayer-book. Unfortunately the king compiled a body of canons for the Northern Church without consultation with the Scottish clergy, and sent it for their acceptance on his own authority. The introduction of this Prayer-book, on July 23, 1637 A.D., in the Cathedral of St. Giles, Edinburgh, was the signal for a riot. A wild mob collected, broke the windows of the church, and maltreated the clergy, the bishop barely escaping with his life. This was the prelude to a general uprising throughout Scotland, which ended in the rebellion. On March 1, 1638 A.D., the "Solemn League and Covenant" was read aloud in Grey Friars' Church, Edinburgh, and almost universally subscribed. The terms of the document pledged all who assented to it "to effect, without respect of persons, the extirpation of prelacy."

The king, finding a war with Scotland inevitable, was forced to summon Parliament in order to obtain subsidies. The House, however, declined to treat of supply, and clamoured for a committee of religion. Charles thereupon dissolved, after a month's session, what is called the "Short Parliament." Laud was unfairly and falsely accused of advising the king to take this step, and a mob of five hundred ruffians attacked Lambeth Palace;

but the archbishop, having been forewarned, took measures to repel them.

According to custom, Convocation should have been dissolved concurrently with Parliament. Now, however, Convocation continued to sit, Laud's hands being strengthened by a new writ authorising the members to act as a synod in order to vote money for the king's necessities and to make new canons, one of which was intended to prevent Scotch disaffection from spreading into England by imposing an oath on the clergy that they would approve and maintain the doctrine, discipline, and government of the Church of England. The "et cetera" clause in this oath (being merely an abbreviation for the list of Church officials) was regarded as implying some secret popish design, and led to such discontent (accentuated by the defeat of the royal forces by the Scotch) that the king was compelled to summon, on November 3, 1640 A.D., what is known as the "Long Parliament," the title referring to the fact that it sat continuously for nearly twenty years, until March, 1660 A.D. It has been described as the most bloodthirsty tribunal that ever assembled until the period of the French Revolution. One of its first acts was to impeach Strafford for treason. Failing to condemn him legally, the Commons, in their vindictive hate, proceeded against him by the method of impeachment, and he was beheaded on May 12, 1641 A.D.

The faith that Laud always had in dreams and omens is remarkable. He mentions his dreams as if they were matters of importance, and seems sometimes to regard them as almost prophetical. They are mentioned in his diary, and often with some exclamation, such as "God grant better things!" He tells how, on his entering the guard-room at Lambeth Palace a few days before his foes proceeded to extremities against him, he found that the cord by which his portrait was suspended had broken, and the picture was lying face downwards on the floor, and he added the note, " God grant this be not a bad omen!"

The toils of his enemies were now rapidly closing round the archbishop. On December 18, 1640 A.D., he was by the House of Commons denounced as a traitor, and committed to the custody of the gentleman usher of the Black Rod. In the February following he was brought up to the House of Lords to hear the articles of impeachment read aloud. His speech in defence is powerful and pathetic. What grieved him most and roused his indignation was the charge of unfaithfulness to the Church. He was committed to the Tower on March 1, 1641 A.D.

The next movement of the Puritan revolutionists was to impeach thirteen prelates for the part they took in promulgating the late canons. On February 6, 1642 A.D., a Bill was passed excluding the bishops from the Upper House and depriving them of all authority. Charles in his weakness gave his consent to this measure, as he had acquiesced in the murder of Strafford.

For nearly three years the archbishop, an old man of seventy years, bowed down with the cares and anxieties of his life, in enfeebled health, deprived of the companionship of friends or the solace of books, was kept a prisoner, and not even allowed to send for money to provide the simplest comforts. In vain did he appeal to the House to allow his trial to proceed. His enemies pursued him with malignant hatred, but as they were unable to find evidence against him they dared not bring their accusations to an issue. His trial began in November, 1643 A.D., and did not conclude till the following October. During that period he was subjected to the vilest insults and abuse that petty spitefulness could invent. On November 13, 1644 A.D., he was voted by the House of Commons to be guilty of high treason. Six peers only attended to pass the Bill of attainder in the Upper House. He was beheaded on Tower Hill on January 10, 1645 A.D.

Thus died—should we not rather say, thus was shamefully and foully murdered?—a man who has shed a lustre on the high and sacred office which he held. That Laud was despotic no one will deny, but he exerted his powers to enforce (without overstepping) the law upon those who had sworn to observe and keep it. He was a loyal and devoted son of the Church of England, which owes much to his loving and fearless labours. Nothing can extenuate or excuse the malice, the injustice, or the perjury of those who, in their littleness and fanaticism, raved against one whose superiority, religious as well as moral, bred in them envy, hatred, and malice. He has been well described as "a man who could and did make great mistakes, but who never knowingly chose the lower part."

CHAPTER X.

WILLIAM SANCROFT (1678-1693 A.D.).

ON the same day that the Lords passed the ordinance of attainder against the Archbishop of Canterbury, William Laud, they likewise passed an ordinance for the abolition of the Book of Common Prayer, and for establishing the "Directory of Public Worship," in which rules were laid down for the conduct of religious services without liturgy or formulæ of any kind. This attack upon the doctrines of the Church, together with the shameful and lawless execution of the archbishop, was rapidly followed by an assualt upon the monarchy. Whatever may have been the vacillation and weakness of King Charles I., it must be remembered that on one point he remained firm. Up to the last he might have saved his life, if only he would have consented to the establishment of Presbyterianism as the national religion. But he absolutely and resolutely declined to place the Anglican Church on a level with sectarianism. "I am firm," he said, "to Primitive Episcopacy, not to have it extirpated if I can hinder it." And again, "I have done what I could to bring my conscience to a compliance with their proposals, and cannot, and I will not lose my conscience to save my life."

The five years which succeeded the murder of the king formed a period of wild religious anarchy, during which every indignity and persecution that could be devised were heaped upon the clergy. Not only were they turned out of their livings, but in November, 1655 A.D., Oliver Cromwell, who has been described as a model of Christian tolerance, issued an edict prohibiting the employment of those clergy who had been ejected or sequestered, of fellows of colleges, or schoolmasters; and ruling that no such persons were to engage in tuition, serve as chaplains, or administer the sacraments.

And yet, in spite of the tyranny of the Puritan fanatics, who had temporarily usurped the power of government, there were certain priests who openly performed the duties to which they had been ordained, in defiance of these unrighteous edicts. As late as Christmas Day, 1657 A.D., John Evelyn was present at a celebration of the Holy Communion in Exeter Chapel, London, which was interrupted by an invasion of soldiery, who levelled their muskets at the communicants, "as if they would have shot us at the altar." Another instance of courageous defiance of the orders of the usurping Parliament is shown in the conduct of the Rev. George Bate, Rector of Maidsmorton, in Buckinghamshire, who christened children, and performed the marriage ceremony according to the rites of the Church of England, during the whole of the Protectorate of Cromwell.

On the restoration of Charles II. the Church and

her clergy resumed their position and functions. The Savoy Conference, which was an unsuccessful attempt to bring about a compromise between Anglicanism and Presbyterianism, was followed by a careful revision of the Prayer-book, 1662 A.D. Though as many as six hundred verbal and other alterations were made, the majority of them were of no doctrinal significance, nor did they materially change the character of the liturgy, which was then cast into the exact form which we use at the present day.

Notwithstanding the prevalence of immorality at the court of Charles II., the position of the Church of England, and her influence over the nation, made steady advance, although this was in some measure checked by the rise of Latitudinarianism towards the close of this reign.

William Juxon, Bishop of London, who attended Charles I. at his execution, was made Archbishop of Canterbury at the Restoration, the see having been vacant since the death of Laud. He died in 1663 A.D., and was succeeded by Gilbert Sheldon, who held the primacy for fourteen years.

William Sancroft, the next archbishop, was born at Fressingfield, in Suffolk, in 1616 A.D. In due course he went up to Cambridge, where he entered at Emmanuel College, becoming a Fellow of the college in 1642 A.D. The following year, under pressure from the Scotch Covenanters, the "Solemn League and Covenant" (pledging those who subscribed it to effect, "without respect of persons, the extirpation of prelacy") was forced upon the nation (*i.e.* on all persons above the age of eighteen) by order of Parliament. Sancroft's refusal to sign the document caused him to lose his Fellowship.

For several years he travelled in France and Italy, where he acquired some valuable knowledge of the political conditions of European countries, and also devoted himself to theological studies. Returning to England at the Restoration, Sancroft was almost immediately appointed University Preacher, and two years later was elected Master of Emmanuel College. In 1663 A.D. he became Dean of York, and the following year he was transferred to St. Paul's.

A vast sum of money had been raised and expended on the restoration of old St. Paul's before the rebellion broke out, but the triumph of the Puritans stopped the work, and the money that remained was seized and confiscated, so that the cathedral church was neglected and damaged to such an extent as to reduce it to the ruined condition into which it had fallen before the episcopate of Laud.

The first work of the new dean was to take steps to restore the old Gothic church, but the disastrous plague of the next year frustrated his designs. In Evelyn's diary of August 27, 1666 A.D., we find the following entry: "I went to St. Paul's Church, where, with Dr. Wren, the Bishop of London, the Dean of St. Paul's, and others, with several expert workmen, we went about to survey the general decays of that ancient and venerable church, and to set down in writing the particulars of what was fit to be done with the charge thereof. . . . We had a mind to build the steeple with a noble cupola, a form of church-building not as yet known in England, but of wonderful grace." Unfortunately the Great Fire of London, which broke out the following week, reduced the cathedral to a heap of rubbish.

Without delay the Dean of St. Paul's, together with the Archbishop of Canterbury and the Bishop of London, decided on producing, with a view to its restoration, "a design, handsome and noble, and suitable to all the ends of it, and to the reputation of the city and nation, and to take it for granted that money will be had to accomplish it." The proposal was communicated to Dr. Christopher Wren, then Professor of Astronomy at Oxford, and the dean contributed liberally towards the carrying out of the plan.

In November, 1677 A.D., Archbishop Sheldon died, and Dean Sancroft was promoted to the primacy over the heads of all the bishops. He was a devoted Churchman, sincere and earnest, and a good administrator. Though it is probable that he owed his appointment largely to the influence of the Duke of York, yet he gave proof of the independence of his character by seeking an interview with the king's brother, shortly after his elevation to the primacy, when he earnestly exhorted the duke to abandon the Romish religion, and be reconciled to the Church of England.

The next few years were chiefly remarkable for the plots to kill the king. The most notable of these were the popish conspiracy, real or imaginary, to introduce papal authority, revealed by Titus Oates in 1678 A.D., which was answered by a new

Test Act, excluding Romanists from sitting in either House of Parliament; and the Rye House plot in 1683 A.D., for alleged complicity in which Lord Russell and Algernon Sidney were executed.

On February 6, 1685 A.D., King Charles II. died, after a brief sickness. Up to the last his real religious convictions were unknown. He was attended during his last hours by several of the bishops. Archbishop Sancroft, we are told, "made a weighty exhortation to him, in which he used a good degree of freedom," while the saintly Bishop Ken "applied himself much to the awaking the king's conscience." But the king refused to receive the Holy Communion, and it is said that a Romanist priest named Huddleston, who had assisted Charles in his escape after the battle of Worcester, was smuggled into his presence to administer to him the last rites of the Roman Church.

The Duke of York, who succeeded his brother on the throne as James II., hastened to pledge himself to defend and support the National Church, although he took the earliest opportunity of demonstrating that he did not intend to withhold his allegiance from the Church of Rome, by publicly attending "Mass." The archbishop has been blamed for consenting to the command that at the coronation he should omit the Communion Service and the ceremony of presenting the sovereign with an English translation of the Bible. But this course was at least more reverent than to have allowed the sacrament to be profaned by insisting on its reception by one who did not hesitate to regard it with contempt.

The king's avowed partiality to the Church of Rome, the severity and barbarity of his treatment of the prisoners captured in Monmouth's rebellion, and his persecution of Presbyterians and Nonconformists, all tended to increase his unpopularity. But he had prorogued Parliament, and had no intention of calling it together again. The courts of law were his obsequious tools. There was only one power in the State from which he had anything to fear, and that power was the Church of England. It was the Church which, at this critical juncture, saved the liberties of the country. The London pulpits rang with denunciations of Romanism, and the cry was taken up, and pamphlets issued, in every part of the land. Whereupon the king used his power as supreme ordinary to prohibit preaching on controverted points of doctrine. The disregard of this injunction by Dr. Sharp, Dean of Norwich and Rector of St. Giles', and the support which the dean received from Dr. Compton, Bishop of London, against whom the king's anger was consequently turned, gave rise to the following important consequences.

The High Commission Court of Queen Elizabeth, which had made itself specially obnoxious to the Puritans during the primacy of Laud, had been abolished in July, 1641 A.D. The accession of Charles II. had reinstated such spiritual tribunals as the Court of Arches, the Consistory Courts, etc., but he declared the High Commission Court incapable of existence. James II., in defiance of the Act, reconstituted it, to consist of four laymen and three bishops, the primate being appointed one of the episcopal commissioners. But although Sancroft, whose loyalty and respect for the kingly office were almost a second nature to him, declined to take part in proceedings which were absolutely illegal, and manifestly designed to compass the ruin of the Church, it is a matter of surprise and regret that he should have asked to be excused merely on the plea of ill-health and numerous engagements, more especially as there exist documents in his own handwriting, proving the constitution of the court to be contrary to law, and we know, from his subsequent conduct, that he was certainly not devoid of courage. By a most shameless process of intimidation, the king obtained a majority on the commission for the condemnation of the Bishop of London, who was suspended from the exercise of his office.

Finding himself unable to bend the loyalist clergy to his will, James determined to effect a great coalition of Romanists and Dissenters. In April, 1687 A.D., he published a "Declaration for Liberty of Conscience," suspending all penal statutes against Romanists and Dissenters, abolishing religious tests, and pardoning all who were undergoing penalties for their peculiar beliefs. But this *ruse* did not succeed. The clergy were roused to indignation, while many of the leading Nonconformists joined with them in denouncing the document as insidious and illegal.

The king thereupon resolved to precipitate a crisis by republishing on May 4, 1688 A.D., the above-mentioned "Declaration," appending thereto an order that the bishops were to cause it to be read in all the churches and chapels throughout their dioceses.

The primate at once showed himself fully equal to the occasion, and took a decided line against the unconstitutional and humiliating course which the royal injunction imposed upon the Church. He summoned the most eminent of the London clergy to meet him at Lambeth, and wrote a circular to the bishops earnestly desiring them to come with all possible speed. After careful deliberation, it was unanimously decided that it was expedient that the clergy should not publish the Declaration. Having come to this determination, a petition to the king was drawn up, stating that the "Declaration is founded upon such a dispensing power as hath been often declared illegal in Parliament . . . ; and is a matter of so great moment and consequence to the whole nation, both in Church and State, that your petitioners cannot in prudence, honour, or conscience, so far make themselves parties to it, as the distribution of it all over the nation, and the solemn publication of it once and again, even in God's house, must amount to in common and reasonable construction." The petition was written in the archbishop's own hand, and signed by himself and the following six bishops, viz. Lloyd of St. Asaph, Turner of Ely, Lake of Chichester, Ken of Bath and Wells, White of Peterborough, and Trelawney of Bristol. Six other bishops, viz. London, Norwich, Gloucester, Salisbury, Winchester, and Exeter, appended an "approbo" with their signatures during the following week.

It was late in the evening of May 18 when this

petition was finally drawn up. As the Declaration was ordered to be read in the churches on May 20, no time was to be lost. The six bishops arrived at Whitehall at ten o'clock at night, and requested an interview with the king. Sancroft did not accompany them, as he had been struck off the Privy Council, and forbidden to appear at Court, since his refusal to act on the High Commission Court.

The king readily admitted the bishops, anticipating a petition of a very different character. When he read the document he expressed himself both astonished and irritated. As he folded it up he exclaimed, "Here are strange words. This is a standard of rebellion. I did not expect such usage from the Church of England." On Sunday, May 20, only four incumbents throughout the whole of London read the Declaration. Bishop Sprat of Rochester, who was also Dean of Westminster, read it in the Abbey, but the congregation had dispersed before he could finish. Throughout the country the clergy followed the example of their London brethren, and less than two hundred incumbents (out of ten thousand) promulgated the hateful document.

It was not to be supposed that James, who was known to be a man of obstinate temper, would allow the matter to drop. Accordingly, on the evening of May 27, the archbishop and his six co-signatories were summoned to appear on June 8 before his Majesty in Council. Acting on the advice of the Lord Chancellor, Jeffries, the king made the petition the ground for an action for libel. The bishops pleaded their privileges as peers, and refused to enter into recognisances. They were thereupon committed to the Tower. The public excitement was intense, the river-banks (it being considered safer, in view of the strong popular feeling, to convey them by water than through the streets) being thronged by a sympathetic crowd. Their prison was attended like the presence-chamber of royalty, and the trial at Westminster, which was held on June 29, is said to have been witnessed by half the nobility of England. When at ten o'clock the next morning the jury returned into court with a verdict of "Not Guilty," the enthusiasm of the nation was indescribable. Congratulations poured in to the primate from all quarters, the most significant of which were those from William of Orange, the king's son-in-law, and from the Presbyterians of Scotland.

The same day a document was despatched inviting the Prince of Orange to come over to the assistance of the Church and nation. While the bishops and many leading Churchmen, strong in their support of the principle of Divine right, desired no more that that William should act as regent, the national sentiment was in favour of James's deposition. On September 30 William issued a declaration that, as husband of Mary, he was coming with an army to uphold the "Protestant religion." At length the king realized his danger, and in his extremity he sought counsel of the bishops, and attempted to conciliate the Church. By the advice of the prelates he dissolved the High Commission Court, reinstated the Fellows of Magdalen College, Oxford, whom he had illegally ejected, and removed the Romanists from the Privy Council; but he declined to yield his claim to the power of dispensing with the laws, and refused to call Parliament together. William's manifesto, stating that he came at the request of the lords spiritual and temporal, was placed in James's hands. Sancroft and the other bishops indignantly vindicated the loyalty of the bench, but would not sign a "Declaration of Abhorrence" against William's expedition. The Prince of Orange landed at Torbay on November 5, and marched unopposed to Exeter; whereupon the king, finding himself deserted on all hands, took safety in flight. A Convention Parliament was summoned, met on January 22, 1689 A.D., and declared that, as James had deserted the nation, the throne should be settled on William and Mary as joint rulers. On February 13 they were crowned king and queen.

In the deliberations of the house of Lords at this time there was much division of opinion. The venerable primate, who should at all costs have given the benefit of his valuable counsel, absented himself, in spite of urgent invitations, from all their deliberations.

He felt deeply the difficult position in which he, with the bishops and clergy, was placed. King James, who despised and delighted to humiliate them, was the sovereign to whom they had sworn allegiance. Could they, although they knew that to support him would be to endanger the Church, so far transgress their oath of allegiance as to support the Dutch prince in opposition to their lawful monarch? The appointment of William as regent commended itself to them as a compromise, but Parliament vetoed the proposal (insisting that William should be king or nothing), and required a new oath of allegiance to William and Mary, which was to be taken by August 1. The archbishop, together with Bishops Ken, Turner, Frampton, Lloyd, White, Thomas, Lake, and Cartwright, and about four hundred of the clergy, refused to comply, and were relegated to poverty and disgrace.

These Nonjurors, as they were called, though small in numbers, included some of the most saintly and energetic of the prelates, and some of the most learned and highly gifted of the Church's divines.

The aged primate, having declined to take the oath, still remained at Lambeth, and, by the forbearance of the Government, was allowed to continue in possession, keeping up his full archiepiscopal state, until October, 1690.

At length he was compelled by process of law to leave Lambeth. He retired to his native place, Fressingfield, where he lived contentedly and cheerfully on £50 a year. He died on November 24, 1693 A.D.

The character of Archbishop Sancroft is somewhat complex. He was a devoted Churchman, and a zealous guardian of the Church's doctrine and rights. His desire to avoid strife led him, on more than one occasion, to lay himself open to the charge of pusillanimity and vacillation. But when a clear question of principle was at stake, his courage and firmness were unshakable. His pilotage of the Church of England, at one of the most critical periods of her history, has earned for his memory the gratitude and affection of all true lovers of the Anglican Church.

ARCHBISHOP WHITGIFT.
By permission of His Grace the Archbishop of Canterbury.
FROM THE ORIGINAL PICTURE IN LAMBETH PALACE.

CHAPTER XI.

WILLIAM HOWLEY (1828-1848 A.D.).

SANCROFT was succeeded in the primacy by Tillotson, Dean of St. Paul's, who, on the deprivation of the Nonjuring bishops, was promoted to the archbishopric of Canterbury. Tillotson and Burnet, Bishop of Salisbury, may be regarded as the two chief divines of the Latitudinarian School.

The reign of William and Mary is chiefly noticeable for the endeavour to bring about a "good agreement between the Church of England and all Protestant Dissenters." With this end in view, the "Toleration Bill" was passed in March, 1689 A.D., relieving dissenting laymen from the pressure of those Acts which had made absence from Divine service a crime. The "Bill for Union," providing for the admission of Presbyterian ministers to Church preferment, was, however, rejected by the House of Commons, who desired the matter to be referred to Convocation. The synod was accordingly summoned, and firmly opposed the revolutionary measures brought forward by the king. In consequence of the action of the Lower House, Convocation was silenced for ten years, till 1701 A.D. The members were again cited to meet during the reign of Queen Anne; but in 1717 A.D., under George I., the renewal of the licence for the transaction of business was refused, although the Convocation was always summoned with Parliament, passed a dutiful address to the Crown, and was adjourned. Thus, for one hundred and thirty-seven years, the deliberative representative assembly of the Church of England was practically suppressed.

The reigns of the four Georges are conterminous with the condition of stagnation in the life of the Church of England. The Lutheran proclivities of George I., combined with his immoral life, augured ill for any efforts on his part on behalf of the Anglican Church. The latitudinarianism and erastianism of the bishops, the spread of heresy (chiefly with respect to the doctrine of the Trinity) among Dissenters, and to some extent also among Churchmen, and the prevalence of religious indifference among all classes, mark out the eighteenth century as one of the saddest epochs of the Church's history.

This state of things is accountable for the rise and success of Methodism. The founder of this system lived and died a devoted son of the Church of England, in spite of her apathy and spiritual deadness. At the present day, when the sect which bears the name of Wesley, and the smaller bodies that have seceded from it, take up a position of independence, and sometimes even of hostility, to the Church which they deserted, the origin of Methodism is obscured and misunderstood. John Wesley desired nothing more than to awaken and stir up a spirit of religious enthusiasm within the Church, and the enormous influence which he wielded, and the quickening of spiritual fervour which resulted from his efforts, saved the country from relapsing into a state of dead unbelief. Strange as it may seem, the Methodist revival laid the foundation for the Tractarian movement, although they approached the same end by such very different processes. The latter has been described as "not antagonistic but supplemental" to the former, "holding quite as strongly the necessity of conversion, justification by faith, and the supremacy of the Scriptures; but also bringing into prominence those doctrines which had been somewhat undervalued, viz. the doctrine of the sacraments, of faith showing itself by works, of Church authority, and the Apostolical succession."

When John Wesley was at the height of his popularity, William Howley was born, in 1765 A.D. He was the son of the Vicar of Ropley, in Hampshire, a small parish about ten miles from Winchester, and was educated at the historic school founded by William of Wykeham. Thence he went to Oxford, where he had a distinguished career, being appointed Regius Professor of Divinity at his University in 1809 A.D.

Four years later, in 1813 A.D., William Howley was promoted to the bishopric of London. In his Primary Visitation Charge the following year he gives us an insight into the character and reputation of the clergy, at a time when the improvement in the administration of ecclesiastical affairs was beginning to show itself. He speaks of them as being "respected and respectable as a body for piety, for learning, and conscientious attention to their pastoral care, and abounding with members distinguished in an eminent degree by all the qualifications which bestow attraction or dignity on intrinsic worth;" and five years later he confirms the opinion he then held. "A body," he says, "more truly respectable for learning and piety than the clergy of this diocese will not easily be found."

In 1828 A.D. the Duke of Wellington, who was then Prime Minister, nominated the Bishop of London for the primacy, and Dr. Howley became the eighty-eighth Archbishop of Canterbury. One of his earliest public acts after his appointment was to take up a position antagonistic to the Government on the Roman Catholic Emancipation Act, which, however, was passed in April, 1829 A.D.

Although his strong Conservative principles led him to offer a strong opposition to the great Reform Bill of 1832 A.D., he co-operated cordially with the Whig Government in the foundation of the Ecclesiastical Commission. The removal of the disabilities attaching to various religious bodies outside the National Church, which Parliament had effected by slow gradations, had led to a series of determined attacks upon her by these emancipated sects. They sought to benefit themselves at her expense. So loud was the clamour, and so persistent were the fabrications circulated as to the fabulous wealth of the Church, that in 1831 A.D. a Royal Commission was appointed to inquire into and report upon the exact condition of the ecclesiastical revenues. There were many anomalies in the then existing distribution of these revenues which were seen to require modification and readjustment, and accordingly, in 1836 A.D., the Ecclesiastical Commissioners, with the Archbishop of Canterbury at the head, were incorporated as a permanent body to deal with the estates belonging to the cathedral bodies, and (after setting aside a sum sufficient for the payment of specified incomes to the bishops and the deans and chapters, and for providing for them suitable residences) to apply the residue to the augmentation of poor livings and the endowment of new parishes in populous districts.

King George IV., who died June 26, 1830 A.D., was succeeded by his brother, William IV., who reigned for seven years. The coronation service was performed by Archbishop Howley, who also officiated at the coronation of Queen Victoria on June 28, 1838 A.D., a year after her accession.

The archbishop was one of the first of her subjects whom the young queen saw after she had so unexpectedly attained to her new position. The following narrative will be of interest:—" The Archbishop of Canterbury, Dr. Howley, and the Lord Chamberlain, the Marquis of Conyngham, left Windsor for Kensington Palace, where the Princess Victoria had been residing, to inform her of the king's death. It was two hours after midnight when they started, and they did not reach Kensington until five o'clock in the morning. They knocked, they rang, they thumped for a considerable time, before they could rouse the porter at the gate; they were again kept waiting in the courtyard, then turned into one of the lower rooms, where they seemed forgotten by everybody. They rang the bell, and desired that the attendant of the Princess Victoria might be sent to inform her Royal Highness that they requested an audience on business of importance. After another delay, and another ringing to inquire the cause, the attendant was summoned, who stated that the princess was in such a sweet sleep that she could not venture to disturb her. Then they said, 'We are come on business of State to the queen, and even her sleep must give way to that.' It did; and to prove that she did not keep them waiting, in a few minutes she came into the room in a loose white nightgown and shawl, her nightcap thrown off, and her hair falling upon her shoulders, her feet in slippers, tears in her eyes, but perfectly collected and dignified."

Soon after Bishop Howley's translation to the primacy, the Oxford movement, as it has been called, sprang into existence. The dangers which apparently threatened the Church, due partly to the indifference and hostility of ministers of State, and partly to the attacks of Dissenters and Romanists, were responsible for the formation, in 1833 A.D., of an "Association of Friends of the Church." This was inaugurated through the initiative of the Rev. Hugh James Rose, who was chosen by the archbishop as his domestic chaplain and confidential friend. The objects of the Association, as drawn up at the Hadleigh Conference, were "(1) To maintain inviolate the doctrines, the services, and the discipline of the Church; and (2) to afford Churchmen an opportunity of exchanging their sentiments, and co-operating together on a large scale." An address to the Archbishop of Canterbury, drawn up by Mr. Palmer, was signed by about seven thousand clergy, and presented in the Library of Lambeth Palace on February 5, 1834 A.D. It was couched in vague terms, but its purport was to deplore the growth of latitudinarian sentiments, and the prevalent ignorance concerning the spiritual claims of the Church, and to express the assurance, on the part of the signatories, of their devoted adherence to the Apostolical doctrine and polity of the Church, and their deep-rooted attachment to her venerable liturgy. His Grace received it with much courtesy, saying that he "anticipated good effects from this public declaration of the sentiments of the clergy." He added that he "regarded it as a direct contradiction of misrepresentation and falsehood of different kinds which have been widely circulated, as an avowal of your unshaken adherence to our National Church, its faith, and its formularies, and as a testimony of your veneration for the episcopal office, and of your cordial respect for your bishops."

A similar address, prepared by the laity, and signed by two hundred and thirty thousand heads of families, was presented to the archbishop the following May. These two documents, and the address to the king which was subsequently forwarded, had a marked effect in bringing about a reaction throughout the country in favour of the Church of England, and in preparing the way for the deepening of the spiritual life of the nation, which has made such vast progress during the last half-century.

The Tractarian movement, after exciting a vast amount of public attention for several years, reached its culminating point with the issue of Tract 90, in 1841 A.D. Although the archbishop maintained a keen interest in the progress of the controversy, and during the early years (until 1838 A.D.) was brought into close touch with every development of it through his chaplain, the Rev. H. J. Rose, his natural timidity of character, or, to speak more correctly, his retiring disposition, prevented him from taking a prominent part in the matter, although his sympathies were to a great extent on the side of the Tractarians.

The same hesitation proved a somewhat unfortunate hindrance to the primate's action in promoting the important Church legislation which marked the commencement of the present reign. The Act for abolishing Pluralities and Non-residence (1 & 2 Vict. c. 106), and the Church Discipline Act (3 & 4 Vict. c. 86), were both indebted to the archbishop in no small measure for the form in which they were finally passed, although his influence was exercised privately rather than publicly.

In 1840 A.D. the Bishop of London (Dr. Blomfield) published a "letter to the Archbishop of Canterbury upon the formation of a fund for endowing additional bishoprics in the Colonies." At that time (twelve years after his accession to the primacy) the number of our colonial and missionary bishoprics was ten. At the present time the number is close upon ninety. The primate sent out invitations for a meeting at Willis's Rooms early in 1841 A.D., which was numerously attended. The meeting resulted in the inauguration of the Colonial Bishoprics Fund, of which the Rt. Hon. W. E. Gladstone was one of the original treasurers, and still holds the office. A large fund was raised, the Society for Promoting Christian Knowledge contributing £10,000, the Society for the Propagation of the Gospel £7500, the Church Missionary Society £600 a year for New Zealand, the Queen Dowager £2000, the Archbishop of Canterbury £1000, and the Bishop of London £1000.

In the same year (1841 A.D.) the archbishop was concerned with the foundation of the bishopric of the United Churches of England and Ireland in Jerusalem. The history of this arrangement is of some interest. The proposal was suggested by the King of Prussia, who made it the subject of a special mission to the Queen of England, and of a particular communication to the primate. His Majesty offered to make a donation of £15,000, yielding an income of £600 a year, for the support of the bishop, who was to be nominated alternately by the Crowns of England and Prussia, the Archbishop of Canterbury having an absolute right of veto. A special Act of Parliament (5 Vict. c. 6) was passed on October 5, 1841 A.D., called the Jerusalem Bishopric Act (under which all our Anglican missionary bishops have since been consecrated), empowering the Archbishops of Canterbury and York, assisted by other bishops, to consecrate British subjects, or the subjects or citizens of any foreign kingdom or state, to be bishops in any foreign country, and, within certain limits, to exercise spiritual jurisdiction over the ministers of British congregations of the United Church of England and Ireland, and over such other Protestant congregations as may be desirous of placing themselves under the authority of such bishops. The prelate so appointed was to be subject to the Archbishop of Canterbury as metropolitan.

Accordingly, Archbishop Howley, having laid the proposal of the King of Prussia before the bishops, proceeded, on November 7, 1841 A.D., to consecrate, in the chapel of Lambeth Palace, the Rev. Michael Solomon Alexander, Hebrew Professor at King's College, London. This action of the archbishop's, although supported by Dr. Hook and other High Churchmen, and the Rev. F. D. Maurice, in the hope that it might be the means of introducing Episcopacy into the Prussian Evangelical body, was strongly opposed by the majority of the High Church party, on the ground that it was an unlawful interference with the Episcopal jurisdiction of the Bishop of the Eastern Church in Jerusalem. Dr. Newman published a formal protest against the action of the primate, and declared that the act of schism—for such he deemed it to be—was one of the final causes which induced him to leave the Church of England. "It was one of the blows," he wrote in his "Apologia," "which broke me."

Four years later Bishop Alexander died, and the King of Prussia nominated Samuel Gobat, a Lutheran divine, who was consecrated in Lambeth Chapel on July 5, 1846 A.D., by the Archbishop of Canterbury, assisted by the Bishops of London, Lichfield, and Calcutta. Since the death of Dr. Gobat's successor, Bishop Barclay, in 1881 A.D., the Prussian arrangement has lapsed, and the present bishop is supported by our Anglican Church Societies, and appointed by the primate.

Towards the close of Archbishop Howley's life two controversies arose, which excited much feeling at the time. The first of these had reference to Dr. Hampden, the second to the Rev. G. C. Gorham.

Hampden was tutor of Oriel College, Oxford, and in 1834 A.D. he published a pamphlet on the admission of Dissenters to the University, in which "Socinians are placed on a level with other Christians." To the astonishment and disgust of the University, he was nominated Regius Professor of Divinity by the Government two years later. A band of zealous Churchmen succeeded in obtaining, in the Convocation of the University of Oxford (by a majority of 474 votes to 94), a censure of the new professor. In 1847 A.D. Lord John Russell nominated Hampden to the bishopric of Hereford. A remonstrance addressed to the Prime Minister by thirteen bishops and a large number of the clergy was ignored. When the election to the see of Hereford was "confirmed" in Bow Church, the objectors made their protest, but this was ruled out of order. The last hope of those who opposed the appointment rested in the primate, who might refuse to consecrate. But at this juncture Archbishop Howley died, and his successor shortly afterwards, on March 26, 1848 A.D., consecrated Dr. Hampden in Lambeth Chapel.

The other controversy above referred to was that which arose in the case of the Rev. G. C. Gorham. This clergyman was, in June, 1847 A.D., presented by the Lord Chancellor to the living of Brampford Speke, in the diocese of Exeter. The bishop of the diocese refused to institute him, on the ground that he was unsound in doctrine in denying that regeneration is in all cases wrought by baptism. Mr. Gorham appealed to the Court of Arches, but the judgment which upheld the bishop's decision was not delivered until 1849 A.D. The Privy Council afterwards reversed the ruling of the Arches Court in favour of Mr. Gorham.

Archbishop Howley took an active part in maintaining the religious instruction in elementary schools. Until the Education Act of 1870 A.D., the education of the children of the poor had been carried out almost entirely by the Church, during the eighteenth century by the Society for Promoting Christian Knowledge, and after 1811 A.D. by the "**National** Society for Promoting the Education of the Poor in the Principles of the Established Church." In 1833 A.D. the House of Commons was persuaded to set aside a grant of £20,000 a year for assisting elementary education in England. Six years later a Committee of Council was formed to administer the grant, and a scheme was proposed by this body which deliberately ignored all distinctive religious teaching, allowing only those children whose parents desired it to have special instruction in Church doctrine, while the rest were to be taught a system that was supposed to include the truths on which all professing Christians were agreed! This scheme was to be introduced into all schools which received a Government grant. It was passed by a majority of five in the House of Commons, but, on the motion of the archbishop, it was defeated by two to one in the Upper House.

The archbishop possessed considerable architectural taste, and throughout his life he employed his gifts in this direction to good purpose. When Regius Professor of Divinity at Oxford he rebuilt the professor's house. After his appointment to the see of London, he set to work to reconstruct the official residence in St. James's Square, and also considerably renovated Fulham Palace. But his most extensive operations in this respect were carried out at Lambeth. While preserving with appreciative reverence, and carefully restoring, all that was really ancient and historic in the grand old pile, he remorselessly swept away the patchwork jumble which successive primates had added during the preceding century and a half. In place of these he erected, at a cost of about £60,000—half of which came out of his own private purse—the present magnificent range of buildings, extending eastward from Cranmer's Tower, and presenting, both in the main courtyard and in the garden, an imposing battlemented frontage, effectively broken by irregular projections of bay windows and oriels, and relieved by graceful turrets. As soon as these improvements were completed, he undertook the restoration of the chapel, removing the bald high panelling, and substituting for the flat ceiling a lofty groined roof. He also converted the old dining-hall, known as Juxon's Hall, into a library.

The primacy of Archbishop Howley formed the transition period between the new and the old *régime*, and closed the princely days of the archbishopric. Until the formation of the Ecclesiastical

Commission, which fixed the income of the see, the revenues had been very large, and the archbishops had been accustomed to maintain a semi-royal state, and dispense unlimited hospitality.

In the midst of the stir of religious excitement and controversy the archbishop passed peacefully away, after a brief illness, in January, 1848, and was buried on the north side of the chancel in the little church at Addington.

William Howley, who had presided over the see of Canterbury for close upon twenty years, possessed a high order of intellect, and a cultivated mind. He was a finished classic, and a theologian of no mean order. His gentleness of character led him to be always seeking after peace, but behind it was a firmness of purpose which sternly refused to accept a compromise where a matter of principle was involved. During the momentous years of his primacy he controlled the religious movements of the age with such retiring and unassuming power that the fact of his great influence was frequently overlooked. He has been described by Bishop Doane of New Jersey as "the impersonation of Apostolic meekness, sweetening Apostolic dignity." To his active co-operation (as we have seen) was greatly due the rapid increase of the colonial episcopate, and although he was prevented by sickness from taking part in the memorable consecration of five bishops in one day—the Bishops of Barbadoes, Gibraltar, Tasmania, Antigua, and Guiana—on St. Bartholomew's Day, 1842 A.D., in Westminster Abbey, he was able, five years later, to consecrate four bishops at once in the same noble building. At the date of his accession to the primacy there were only five colonial bishoprics. Before his death no less than twenty-two bishops were spread over our colonial empire. It must also be borne in mind that, mainly in consequence of his efforts, his primacy marks the time at which the pulpits of the English Church were first opened to the bishops and clergy of Scotland and America.

His episcopate was an eventful one, and the development of Church life, and the avoidance of many threatened dangers and difficulties, were due in no small degree to the gentle courtesy and loving firmness which were his chief characteristics.

CHAPTER XII.

JOHN BIRD SUMNER (1848–1862 A.D.).

JOHN BIRD SUMNER was born in 1780 A.D. He was the eldest son of the Vicar of Kenilworth, and grandson of the provost of King's College, Cambridge. His early years were spent amid the picturesque and peaceful surroundings of his country home, where, under the influence and teaching of his father, he gained his first insight into the wonders of God's work in nature, which bore such fruit in the researches and writings of his after-life.

At the age of twelve he was sent to Eton, where his career was successful without being specially brilliant. Here he came in contact with many boys whose friendship, once made, continued firm and unvarying. From Eton he proceeded to King's College, Cambridge, where he worked steadily and well, obtaining a scholarship, and later on being elected to a fellowship. He distinguished himself in his studies, becoming Browne's Medallist and Hulsean Prizeman. Taking his B.A. degree in 1802 A.D., he was appointed almost immediately to an assistant-mastership at Eton. The following year, at the age of twenty-three, he was ordained to the diaconate, and within a few months of his ordination he married. In 1815 A.D. Sumner first appeared as an author, the work (which went through many editions) being entitled, "Apostolic Preaching considered in an Examination of St. Paul's Epistles." Within twelve months he published a "Treatise on the Records of the Creation, and on the Moral Attributes of the Creator;" in which, while vindicating the Mosaic account of the creation of the world, he accepted the conclusions of geological science as then understood. This literary effort obtained one of the Burnett prizes, amounting to £400. The book went through seven editions, and was a remarkable testimony at the time to the authority of scientific research. In 1818 A.D. Sumner resigned his mastership at Eton, and became Rector of Mapledurham, in Oxfordshire, a pretty village lying on the high ground between Reading and Henley. Here, in addition to his parochial duties, he persevered in his labours as an author, producing within the next few years a volume on the "Evidences of Christianity derived from its Nature and Reception," a volume of "Sermons on the Christian Faith and Character," and other works which greatly enhanced his fame.

His next piece of preferment was a canonry at Durham. But his tenure of this post was of short duration, for in 1828 A.D. the Duke of Wellington, who was then Prime Minister, recommended him for appointment to the bishopric of Chester. Here he succeeded Dr. Blomfield, who, after having filled the see for four years, was translated to the bishopric of London, in which his twenty-eight years' episcopate was marked with very great power and success.

Sumner's brother, Charles Richard, had also made his mark as a clergyman, having become successively king's chaplain, Bishop of Llandaff, and Dean of St. Paul's in 1826 A.D.; and it is an interesting coincidence that during the same year in which the future Archbishop of Canterbury became Bishop of Chester his brother was promoted to the see of Winchester.

For twenty years John Bird Sumner laboured indefatigably in his northern diocese. At the time of his appointment the see of Chester was regarded almost solely as a stepping-stone to higher preferment. The income was only £1700 a year (while that of the neighbouring diocese of Durham was twenty times as valuable), and it had been the frequent practice of the bishops to hold some rich living at the same time. For example, Bishop Blomfield was Rector of Bishopsgate as well as Bishop of Chester. A few years later, however, after the establishment of the Ecclesiastical Commissioners in 1836 A.D., many of the anomalies in episcopal and parochial incomes were removed, and amongst other changes the stipend of the see of Chester was raised to £4500.

At the time of which we are speaking, shortly before the commencement of the present reign, the want of life and vigour in the Church of England was very marked. She had been greatly weakened by the Wesleyan schism (which took place after Wesley's death, and in opposition to his wishes), a rupture that, in all probability, would never have occurred had the authorities of the Church been capable of adapting themselves to the changed circumstances of the times. As it was, Methodism (to use the term applied at that day to those who adopted and sympathized with the stirring and more emotional system under which the revival within the Church was set on foot) was for a long time regarded with suspicion and disfavour by the bishops and the majority of the parochial clergy. It was not until the breach had become irreparable that the authorities awoke from their lassitude.

Ever since that period there has been a real and rapidly increasing fervour in all ranks of the Church. The enormous increase in the voluntary contributions raised for education and for building and restoring churches, as well as in the development of lay work, have marked the last half-century as one of the brightest annals of our ecclesiastical history. And yet these results did not immediately follow the preaching of Wesley, or perhaps they were delayed and hindered by the schismatic action of his followers, for we find that almost throughout the first half of the present century the parish churches were, speaking generally, in a state of dilapidation and collapse.

As might be expected, the distant dioceses did not feel the effect of the enthusiasm so rapidly as those which were nearer to London. When Bishop Sumner went to Chester in 1828 A.D. he found Church life at a very low ebb. The episcopacy of Bishop Blomfield had not lasted long enough for his influence to have made itself felt in any marked degree. Sumner set himself to work in good earnest, and was instrumental in building churches, founding schools, and arousing, in a variety of ways, a considerable amount of zeal for the work of the Church among the two hundred and fifty-five parishes under his episcopal charge. This was due not only to his activity, but to the deep personal piety which he was universally acknowledged to possess.

His tenure of his northern see was exactly contemporaneous with the primacy of Archbishop Howley, and thus he was brought in contact, as a bishop, with many of the important political and ecclesiastical events which took place during those twenty years. There was the Reform Bill of 1832 A.D., against which the bishops, in the undoubted exercise of their legislative functions, had recorded their votes. Whether in so doing they had acted wisely or unwisely is not a question into which we need here enter. But there is no doubt that the popular outcry against them was both loud and menacing. To quote Bishop Philpotts' celebrated speech: "The bishops were threatened to be driven from their stations because they did not vote for ministers, because for once they had thus voted upon the greatest question agitated since the Revolution, when the bishops had acted in defiance of the Crown. Where would their lordships have been but for the bishops at the Revolution?" Again, there was the establishment of the Ecclesiastical Commissioners, who, in 1836 A.D., were formed into a permanent body for dealing with Church revenues. The Archbishops of Canterbury and York, all the diocesan bishops, five Cabinet ministers, four judges, three deans, and twelve eminent laymen, constitute the Board, which meets every week.

As we saw in the memoir of Archbishop Howley, the Tractarian movement commenced in 1833 A.D. It was not long before almost every bishop was drawn into the controversy. The Bishop of Chester and his brother were both regarded as belonging to the "Evangelical School," and the anti-High Church party looked to them to lead the opposition to what was believed to be a dangerous and Romanizing attack upon the Church. As a matter of fact, the first bishop who definitely condemned the "Tracts" was the future primate, John Bird Sumner. In a later Charge he described the movement as "the work of Satan," and in 1838 A.D. he denounced "the undermining of the foundations of our Protestant Church by men who dwell within her walls," and also protested against the bad faith of those "who sit in the Reformers' seat and traduce the Reformation." Although his views were uncompromisingly those of the "Low Church" party, and the Catholic teaching and practice which it was sought to revive were not only unknown in the English Church, (save to the few who had studied her history and learned what her teaching and practice had been in primitive and mediæval times,) but were branded with the stigma of an affinity to Romanism, one cannot but regret that a prelate of the Church should have allowed himself to make use of such language as has just been quoted in regard to men who were in no degree inferior to himself, either in earnestness of purpose or in spirituality.

The Rev. J. Cave-Browne, in his "History of

Lambeth Palace," thus describes Archbishop Sumner: "He had in early life been credited with a refined scholarship, and had given promise of considerable theological depth and power, especially in the first edition of his 'Apostolic Preaching' (1815). His administration of the see of Chester was marked with more than ordinary zeal and devotion; he was conspicuous as a preacher rather than as a divine; but a tendency, which grew with his advance in years as in dignity, to identify himself with one 'school' rather than to be the 'moderator' of the Church, as his predecessor had been, in days when the two 'schools of thought' were beginning to cause divisions in the Church, led many of those whose views he so vehemently opposed to lose sight of his real worth and earnest piety, and thus, perhaps, to rob him of much of that respect to which his office and his holiness of character entitled him."

It will be remembered that the Gorham controversy (see p. 149) was not concluded when Archbishop Howley died. The judgment of the Privy Council, delivered on March 8, 1850 A.D., in which the new Archbishop of Canterbury, Dr. Sumner, acquiesced, reversed the decision of the Dean of Arches, and laid down that "the doctrine held by Mr. Gorham is not contrary or repugnant to the declared doctrine of the Church of England as by law established, and that Mr. Gorham ought not, by reason of the doctrine held by him, to have been refused admission to the vicarage of Brampford Speke."

Archbishop Sumner thereupon, with a view to

making his position clearer in regard to the doctrine he held about Holy Baptism, republished a work which he had put forward some thirty years before, inserting a new preface, wherein he traced the modification that had taken place in his views on the subject since the book was originally written. This drew from the indefatigable Bishop of Exeter, Dr. Philpotts, who had from the first been uncompromising in his opposition to what he maintained were the unscriptural and heretical views held by Mr. Gorham, a powerful, if somewhat bitter, reply, under the title of "A Letter to the Archbishop of Canterbury from the Bishop of Exeter." The letter thus commences: "I address your Grace under circumstances most unusual, and with feelings the most painful. In the whole history of the Church of England I am not aware that anything of a similar kind has ever before occurred—that the Primate of All England has ever before thrown himself upon the judgment of the world as the writer of a controversial book. Your Grace has been pleased to descend from the exalted position in which your predecessors were, wisely I think, content to stand. You have deemed it your duty to deal publicly with 'a subject' of which you say that 'it has recently become a matter of distressing controversy,' and you will not think it strange if one of the parties in that controversy shall animadvert on the manner in which you deal with it." The bishop proceeds to point out the change which had come over the archbishop's views as to baptism, and adds, "I cannot adequately express my regret that now, in your advanced years, you should materially impair and almost contradict the sounder teaching of your earlier years." He then makes a charge of a far graver character, when he says, "My Lord, you were summoned to attend the hearing of the late cause before the Judicial Committee of Her Majesty's Council, in order that you might assist them in dealing with the questions of doctrine involved in that cause; and I grieve to think that instead of leading you must have misled those whom you were to instruct, not only by misstating the matters on which you advised, but also by misquoting all, or almost all, the authors cited by you in confirmation of your statement." In conclusion the bishop uses these words: "Meanwhile, I have one most painful duty to perform. I have to protest not only against the judgment given in the recent cause, but also against the regular consequences of that judgment. I have to protest against your Grace's doing what you will speedily be called to do, either in person or by some other exercising your authority. I have to protest, and I do hereby solemnly protest before the Church of England, before the Holy Catholic Church, before Him Who is its Divine Head, against your giving mission to exercise cure of souls, within my diocese, to a clergyman who proclaims himself to hold the opinions which Mr. Gorham holds. I protest that any one who gives mission to him till he retract is a favourer and supporter of those heresies. I protest, in conclusion, that I cannot, without sin, and, by God's grace, I will not, hold communion with him, be he who he may, who shall so abuse the high commission which he bears."

The next subject of public importance in connection with the Church, with which Archbishop Sumner was brought into close and definite relationship, was the revival of Convocation. Convocation is practically the Parliament of the Church. There are two Convocations, one of Canterbury and one of York. Each consists of two houses, the Upper House including the bishops of the province, the Lower House being made up of deans, archdeacons, and representatives of the clergy called proctors. Convocation is dissolved and elected with each dissolution and re-election of Parliament. In order to transact important business, the licence of the Crown is required. In 1717 A.D. the licence was refused, because the clergy declined to submit to dictation in matters of faith by the civil power. For one hundred and thirty-seven years the Church's deliberative assembly was silenced, being allowed to meet solely as a matter of form. The earliest attempt at a movement in favour of the revival of the legislative action of Convocation was made in 1826 A.D., but no definite steps were taken. The question of a renewal of synodical action was discussed in 1847 A.D., and in 1850 A.D. a society for the revival of Convocation was set on foot. The following year an important debate on the subject took place in the House of Lords, and when a new Convocation was elected at the General Election of 1852 A.D., it proceeded, fortified by the best legal opinion as to its powers that was obtainable, to apply itself at once to the despatch of business, one of its first acts being to put forward an energetic protest against the new papal hierarchy (which had been established in this country by a papal bull in 1850 A.D.), defining it as "that fresh aggression of the Bishop of Rome, by which he has arrogated to himself the spiritual charge of this nation, thereby denying the existence of that branch of the Church Catholic which was planted in Britain in the primitive ages of Christianity, and has been preserved by a merciful Providence unto this day."

As might be anticipated, the Archbishop of Canterbury was at first opposed to the attempt to revive the synodical action of Convocation. His sympathies were not with the general tendency of the times in such matters, and he was apprehensive, and full of anxiety concerning the possible encouragement that might thus be given to factions and disputes between the High Church and Low Church parties. But he lived long enough to see that his fears were groundless, and before his death he had thrown himself heartily into its deliberations. No words of praise can be too strong to apply to the calm, statesmanlike, and useful discussions which have marked the history of Convocation since it resumed its proper functions. Most of the important Church legislation of the last forty years has either been originated, or has at all events been improved and modified, by Convocation. The northern primate was even more backward in taking action than the Archbishop of Canterbury. But so strong was the popular feeling that the Church was being unfairly treated by the suppression of her powers of deliberation, that it was not long before the Convocation of York followed the example of that of the southern province, and set herself in full working order.

The archbishop soon began, among other things, to be drawn into the difficult and complicated questions arising out of the Ritual disputes and prosecutions which were, directly or indirectly, the outcome of the Tractarian movement. The first of these cases was that of the Hon. and Rev. Robert Liddell, Vicar of St. Paul's, Knightsbridge. Complaint was made against certain points of the ritual at his church, and in December, 1855 A.D., the vicar was ordered, by the Consistory Court of the diocese of London, to make specific alterations. The Court of Arches, on appeal, confirmed this sentence, whereupon Mr. Liddell appealed to her Majesty in Council, with the result that he obtained a ruling more favourable to himself, several of the points raised being decided in accordance with his views. In this judgment, which was delivered on March 21, 1857 A.D., the Archbishop of Canterbury, who, with Bishop Tait, had been specially summoned to the council, concurred.

Three years later the primate was involved in a far more stormy and heated controversy—viz. that which raged around the publication of "Essays and Reviews." The volume was issued in February, 1860 A.D., containing seven articles. The following are the titles, with the names of the authors:—

1. "The Education of the World." By Frederick Temple, D.D., Headmaster of Rugby.

2. "Bunsen's Biblical Researches." By Rowland Williams, D.D.

3. "On the Study of the Evidences of Christianity." By Professor Baden Powell.

4. "The National Church." By the Rev. H. B. Wilson.

5. "On the Mosaic Cosmogony." By Mr. C. W. Goodwin.

6. "Tendencies of Religious Thought in England (1688–1750 A.D.)." By the Rev. Mark Pattison.

7. "On the Interpretation of Scripture." By the Rev. Professor Jowett.

For some months the Essays did not awaken any considerable interest, but a vigorous attack upon them in the *Westminster Review*, followed later by a strong denunciation of the book by the Bishop of Oxford in his autumn Visitation Charge, brought it at once into prominent notice, and enormously increased its circulation.

Addresses and memorials began to pour in upon the archbishop. In February, 1861 A.D., the bishops, at a meeting at Lambeth, decided on replying to one of these memorials in a letter which, when published, might serve as an answer to all. The following is the text of the letter written by the primate, to which the signatures of the Archbishop of York and of twenty-four bishops are appended:—

"I have taken the opportunity of meeting many of my episcopal brethren in London to lay your address before them. They unanimously agree with me in expressing the pain it has given them that any clergyman of our Church should have published such opinions as those concerning which you have addressed me. We cannot understand how these opinions can be held consistently with an honest subscription to the formularies of our Church, with many of the fundamental doctrines of which they appear to us essentially at variance. Whether the language in which these views are expressed is such as to make the publication an act which could be visited in the Ecclesiastical Courts, or to justify the synodical condemnation of the book which contains them, is still under our gravest consideration. But our main hope is our reliance on the blessing of God in the continued and increasing earnestness with which we trust that we and the clergy of our several dioceses may be enabled to teach and preach that good deposit of sound doctrine which our Church teaches in its fulness, and which we pray that she may, by God's grace, ever set forth as the uncorrupted gospel of our Lord Jesus Christ."

The question was shortly afterwards debated at great length in Convocation. On the motion of the Lower House, a committee was appointed to examine and report upon the volume in question. The decision of the committee was embodied in a resolution of the Lower House, that "there are sufficient grounds for proceeding to a synodical judgment upon the book entitled 'Essays and Reviews.'" The Upper House, in view of the fact that two of the Essayists were at that moment being prosecuted in the Ecclesiastical Courts, were in favour of adjourning the consideration of the subject. The ruling of the Court of Arches, which condemned the writers on two of the grounds alleged against them, and sentenced them to a year's suspension, was not pronounced until three months after the archbishop's death. The result of the appeal to the Privy Council will be noticed in the memoir of Archbishop Longley.

Meanwhile the clouds were gathering which

presaged the storm about to burst over the Church in the Colenso controversy, and here, too, the venerable primate was not permitted to see the issue of the struggle. In 1861 A.D., Dr. Colenso, Bishop of Natal, published his "Commentary on the Epistle to the Romans," which Dr. Gray, Bishop of Capetown and Metropolitan, considered to contain many heretical statements. When Bishop Gray was unable to induce the author to withdraw the volume, he wrote to the primate, who thereupon brought the matter before the bishops. Their lordships, while expressing their personal view as to the dangerous tendency of the writer's conclusions, deferred an official examination of the doctrines therein contained pending the arrival in England of the two South African prelates. But the excitement was increased a thousandfold by the issue in the following October (a month after Archbishop Sumner's death) of Dr. Colenso's "The Pentateuch and the Book of Joshua critically examined."

The archbishop had already, when this controversy began, passed the age of eighty, and yet his vigour and activity were unimpaired. He was better fitted for, and perhaps experienced a greater pleasure in, the fulfilment of his pastoral duties than of the wider questions of statesmanship in ecclesiastical matters.

The following words, describing him as he appeared to one of his own clergy, are worth quoting: "His singularly beautiful character has left an image never to be effaced in the memory of all who witnessed it, and that character seemed to have made an impression on his later life. Few will fail to remember the energy and devotion with which, up to the very last, the archbishop entered upon all the duties which the care of the diocese devolved upon him. Up to his latest years he carried on his progresses in the diocese, every part of which was personally known to him ; and when he was urged to intermit in some degree this active oversight, he was accustomed to say that the time would come when he might be unequal to it, but till then he was anxious to continue his personal knowledge of his 'cure.' Travelling in the simplest manner with a single servant, and only distinguished by that graceful dignity which was ever conspicuous in him, he is remembered everywhere as realizing that ideal of the apostolic ministry which he had traced in his earliest and most popular work."

Archbishop Sumner died at Addington Park, after a brief illness, on September 6, 1862 A.D., aged eighty-two years, and was buried in the village churchyard.

He was a ripe scholar, a fluent writer, and a not illiberal thinker, although his sympathies were closely bound up (as we have seen) with the Evangelical school in the Church. But his admirers and his opponents alike combined in praising the justice of his rule, the holiness of his life, and the strength of his example.

CHAPTER XIII.

CHARLES THOMAS LONGLEY (1862–1868 A.D.).

CHARLES THOMAS LONGLEY was the son of John Longley, barrister-at-law and Recorder of Rochester, and was born on July 28, 1794 A.D. He was sent in due course to Westminster School, and then to Christ Church, Oxford, where he graduated in 1815 A.D., taking a first class in classics. He subsequently became college tutor, censor, and public examiner, and was ordained in 1819 A.D.

His first parochial work was undertaken at Cowley, near Oxford, being appointed to this "perpetual curacy" (a technical term for an incumbency, of which the income is derived, not from tithes, but from an annual stipend), in 1823 A.D. About twelve months later he became Rector of West Tytherley, Hampshire, and remained there till 1829 A.D., when he was elected Headmaster of Harrow, receiving his D.D. degree in the same year.

Dr. Longley retained this important position in the educational world until 1836 A.D., when, on his preferment to the episcopal bench, he was succeeded in the headmastership by Christopher Wordsworth, afterwards Bishop of Lincoln.

The first report of the newly inaugurated Ecclesiastical Commission recommended the formation of two new sees in the province of York, viz. Manchester and Ripon. The latter was to cover the West Riding of Yorkshire (with a portion of the North Riding), and the grand old minster church provided a suitable cathedral, the clerical staff of the minster being available as dean and canons. The diocese was constituted by the Act 6 & 7 William IV. c. 79, and Charles Thomas Longley was nominated as its first bishop.

The history of this bishopric is interesting. In Saxon times, as early as the year 678 A.D., Archbishop Theodore, when subdividing the vast diocese of Northumbria, appointed Eadhed to the new see of Ripon; but no successor was elected at his death, and it was then merged in the diocese of York. The minster recalls a long historical retrospect. A church at Ripon is mentioned by the Venerable Bede, said to have been erected by St. Wilfrid in the seventh century. It was originally the church of a monastery, over which the saint presided, and the crypt was known as "St. Wilfrid's Needle." The sacred edifice was rebuilt by Archbishop Roger of York, 1154–1181 A.D., and in the next century Archbishop Gray added the two western towers and the façade which connects them. In 1319 A.D. it was burnt by the Scots; a hundred years later the lantern tower was shattered by a storm; at the close of the sixteenth century the minster was damaged by lightning. It was finally restored by Sir Gilbert Scott in 1861 A.D.

Bishop Longley, after his appointment, at once

set to work to organize and develop Church work in his new diocese, and it is largely owing to his vigour and goodness, and to the thorough foundations which he laid, and the principles of Churchmanship which he inculcated, that the influence of the Church is so strong in the West Riding. Here he laboured for twenty years, until, on the death of Bishop Maltby, he was promoted to the see of Durham. On December 5 he went to Windsor to do homage to the queen. Bishop Tait, who had also been summoned for the same purpose on his appointment as Bishop of London, has the following entry in his diary: "Having been presented by Sir George Grey, I kneeled down on both knees before the queen, just like a little boy at his mother's knee. I placed my joined hands between hers, while she stooped her head so as almost to bend over mine, and I repeated slowly and solemnly the very impressive words of the oath which constitutes the Act of Homage. Longley, the new Bishop of Durham, who had accompanied me, then went through the same ceremony. He had not escaped so quietly from the ceremonial when he was consecrated Bishop of Ripon. His oath was then taken to William IV., and no sooner had he risen from his knees than the king suddenly addressed him in a loud voice, thus: 'Bishop of Ripon, I charge you, as you shall answer before Almighty God, that you never by word or deed give encouragement to those d——d Whigs who would upset the Church of England.'"

After an episcopate of less than four years at Durham, Longley was translated, on the death of

Dr. Musgrave, to the archbishopric of York. He had only occupied the northern primacy for two years, when, on the death of Archbishop Sumner, on September 6, 1862 A.D., he was once again promoted, and became Archbishop of Canterbury.

Two important controversies were at that time raging within the Church of England, and both came almost immediately before the new primate in an official way.

1. The first of these was the prosecution of two of the contributors (Dr. Rowland Williams and the Rev. H. B. Wilson) to "Essays and Reviews." The judgment of the Dean of Arches, which sentenced them to a year's suspension, was delivered on December 15, 1862 A.D. Both were condemned for denying, either directly or by implication, the inspiration of Holy Scripture, and Mr. Wilson for denying the eternity of future punishment. The Judicial Committee of the Privy Council, to whom they appealed, consisted of the Archbishop of Canterbury (Dr. Longley), the Archbishop of York (Dr. Thomson), both just appointed, the Bishop of London (Dr. Tait), the Lord Chancellor, and three lay judges. The case was heard in June, 1863 A.D., but judgment was not given till the following February. The decision, which reviewed the whole matter at considerable length, ended with these words: "On the short extracts before us, our judgment is that the charges are not proved." From this ruling the two archbishops dissented, and shortly afterwards each published a pastoral letter, explaining his position in the matter, and the grounds on which he disagreed with his colleagues.

In March, 1864 A.D., a deputation waited on the two archbishops at Lambeth Palace, to present an address signed by no less than one hundred and thirty-seven thousand lay members of the Church of England, expressing their gratitude to the primates for the action they had taken in declining to acquiesce in the decision of the Privy Council. Meantime the full tide of the wrath of both clergy and laity was turned upon Bishop Tait, who had supported the lay judges.

The Convocation of Canterbury met in the following month, and a somewhat heated debate took place in the Upper House, the principal combatants being Bishops Tait and Thirlwall (of St. David's) on one side, and Bishop Wilberforce (of Oxford) on the other. After a protracted discussion, the Bishop of Oxford's motion for the appointment of a committee to examine and report on the volume entitled "Essays and Reviews" was carried by the casting vote of the president (Archbishop Longley). At the next session, in June, 1864 A.D., the committee reported in favour of a synodical condemnation of the book, and this was carried through both Houses. In a debate which took place a few days later in the House of Lords, in which the Lord Chancellor contemptuously referred to the condemnation as illegal, but beneath notice, Bishop Tait, strongly as he had in Convocation opposed the action of his colleagues, now stood forward unflinchingly in support of the privileges of that body, for which firm stand he received the warmest thanks of the archbishop, whose proverbial courtesy and kindliness were sorely tried during the sometimes violent discussions on this burning subject.

2. The second controversy, into the vortex of which the primate was soon drawn, was that of which Dr. Colenso was the central figure.

At the death of Archbishop Sumner, Bishop Colenso's "Commentary on the Epistle to the Romans," and the first part of his work "The Pentateuch and the Book of Joshua critically examined" had been published. The second part of the latter work appeared in January, 1863 A.D.

The primate held a meeting of the bishops the following month, at which their lordships resolved, by a large majority, (1) to advise the Society for the Propagation of the Gospel to "withhold its confidence from the Bishop of Natal until he has been cleared from the charges notoriously incurred by him;" and (2) to inhibit the bishop for the present from preaching in their dioceses.

In consequence of a letter written by Bishop Tait to the archbishop, strongly deprecating the second of the above resolutions, two further meetings were held, and finally an address to Bishop Colenso was drawn up, and signed by forty-one prelates, English, Irish, and Colonial, the only dissentient being the Bishop of St. David's. In this letter the following passages occur:—

"We understand you to say that you do not now believe that which you voluntarily professed to believe, as the indispensable condition of your being intrusted with your present office. We understand you also to say that you have entertained, and have not abandoned, the conviction that you could not use the Ordination Service, inasmuch as in it you 'must require from others a solemn declaration that they "unfeignedly believe all the Canonical Scriptures of the Old and New Testament;" which, with the evidence now before' you, 'it is impossible wholly to believe in.' And we understand you further to intimate that those who think with you are precluded from using the Baptismal Service, and consequently (as we must infer) other offices of the Prayer-book, unless they omit all such passages as assume the truth of the Mosaic history.

"Now, it cannot have escaped you that the inconsistency between the office you hold and the opinions you avow is causing great pain and grievous scandal to the Church. And we solemnly ask you to consider once more, with the most serious attention, whether you can, without harm to your own conscience, retain your position, when you can no longer discharge its duties or use the formularies to which you have subscribed. . . ."

Bishop Colenso wrote in reply, declining to resign his office. The matter was then debated at considerable length in Convocation, but no definite action was taken, pending the result of the trial which was in contemplation. Bishop Gray, the Metropolitan of Cape Town, delivered his judgment on December 16, 1863 A.D., in which he deposed the Bishop of Natal from his office, and inhibited him from exercising his functions within the province. When a protest was raised against the legality of these proceedings, Bishop Gray replied, "I cannot recognize any appeal, except to his Grace the Archbishop of Canterbury." Unfortunately the archbishop, by joining with the other bishops in inhibiting Dr. Colenso from officiating in his diocese, had disqualified himself from hearing the appeal by practically prejudging the case.

Bishop Colenso appealed to the Queen in Council, and the Lord Chancellor delivered judgment in his favour on March 20, 1865 A.D., declaring that "the proceedings taken by the Bishop of Cape Town, and the sentence pronounced by him against the Bishop of Natal, are null and void in law." The Court gave its ruling solely on the question of the legality of the deposition, not on the orthodoxy or otherwise of the writings.

The controversy continued to rage for some time longer, but it assumed a somewhat different phase. Bishop Gray, having satisfied himself in regard to his deposition of his heretical suffragan, was now anxious to press forward the election and consecration of a new bishop for the diocese of Natal. The Archbishop of Canterbury, while recommending caution and thorough inquiry into all the difficulties, was in favour of this step. Further action in the matter was postponed, pending the approaching gathering of the first "Lambeth Conference." This synod, to which all the bishops of the Anglican Communion were invited, and from whose primary meeting under the presidency of Archbishop Longley such benefit has accrued to the Church, is the great event with which the thought of his primacy is associated.

The original suggestion for such an assembly was made as early as September, 1865 A.D., by the provincial synod of the Canadian Church, in which a motion was carried urging upon the Archbishop of Canterbury and the Convocation of his province that means should be adopted "by which the members of our Anglican Communion in all quarters of the world should have a share in the deliberations for her welfare, and be permitted to have a representation in one general council of her members gathered from every land."

The idea was fully debated in Convocation during the following May, the result of the discussions being that the Archbishop of Canterbury was requested to issue an invitation to all the bishops in communion with the Church of England to assemble "for the purpose of Christian sympathy and mutual counsel on matters affecting the welfare of the Church at home and abroad."

Accordingly, on February 22, 1867 A.D., the archbishop wrote to all the bishops of the Anglican Communion—English, Scotch, Irish, Colonial, Missionary, and American—then one hundred and forty-four in number, inviting them to come together at Lambeth Palace on September 24 of the same year, and the three following days. His Grace was careful to define the limits within which the deliberations of the Conference would be restricted. He wrote, "Such a meeting would not be competent to make declarations or lay down definitions on points of doctrine. But united worship and common counsels would greatly tend to maintain practically the unity of the faith, whilst they would bind us in straighter bonds of peace and brotherly charity."

It was feared by several of the bishops at home that such a Conference must almost of necessity increase the confusion already existing in ecclesiastical matters, in consequence of the Colenso controversy and other difficulties, and they therefore determined to absent themselves from the meetings. Among these were the Archbishop of York, and the Bishops of Durham, Carlisle, Ripon, Peterborough, and Manchester. Bishop Thirlwall, of St. David's, at last consented to attend on the understanding, given him privately by the primate, that the question of Bishop Colenso's position should not be introduced or debated.

The Conference met on Tuesday, September 24, 1867 A.D., with a celebration of the Holy Communion in Lambeth Chapel, at which the sermon was preached by Dr. Whitehouse, Bishop of Illinois. The meetings were held in the historic "Guard-room" of the palace, in which hang the portraits of the Archbishops of Canterbury in unbroken succession from Warham, who held the primacy from 1503 to 1533 A.D., to the present day.

In his opening address, Archbishop Longley again laid down, with considerable care, the limits of discussion. "It has never been contemplated," he said, "that we should assume the functions of a general synod of all the Churches in full communion with the Church of England, and take upon ourselves to enact canons that should be binding upon those here represented. We merely propose to discuss matters of practical interest, and pronounce what we deem expedient in resolutions which may serve as safe guides to future action."

It was on the third day that the "burning question" of Bishop Colenso and his opponents became the subject of a heated debate. The introduction of a resolution by Bishop Hopkins, of Vermont (presiding bishop of the American Church), condemning Dr. Colenso as excommunicated, was ruled out of order by the archbishop. The Bishop of St. David's reminded the primate of the understanding that had been previously arrived at, adding, "I throw myself on your Grace's honour and good faith." After a long and animated debate, the archbishop ended the matter by declaring that he did not think it competent to introduce the Natal question except in the guarded way of proposing that a committee be appointed to report on the best mode of delivering the Church from the present scandal. A resolution to this effect was carried by forty-nine votes to ten. The tone of the Conference, and the harmony which had existed, were somewhat marred by the proposal, brought forward at the close of the proceedings by the Bishop of Cape Town, that the meeting should assent to a hypothetical resolution passed by the Convocation of Canterbury in June, 1866 A.D., in regard to the appointment of a new Bishop of Natal.

The archbishop, whose courteous bearing and unruffled temper contributed so much to the success of the Conference, was unable to restrain the excitement that prevailed, and was powerless to prevent, as he undoubtedly desired to do, a decision being arrived at which to a great extent stultified his previous ruling.

The closing service was held on Saturday, September 28, in Lambeth Parish Church, the sermon being preached by Bishop Fulford of Montreal.

The various committees appointed by the synod continued their labours through the autumn, and on December 10, a final meeting of the bishops who were still in England was held at Lambeth to receive the reports.

An interesting sequel to the Conference took place a few years later, when a massive alms-basin was presented to the Archbishop of Canterbury (no longer Dr. Longley, but his successor, Dr. Tait), as a memorial gift from the bishops of the American Church. The design is a very beautiful one. In the centre is the hemisphere, showing the Atlantic Ocean, with the Old World on the east of it, and the New World on the west. A scroll on the ocean bears the inscription, "*Orbis veteri novus, occidens orienti, filia matri*" ("The new world to the old, the west to the east, the daughter to the mother"). Various symbolic designs are traceable both in the dish itself and round the rim. The presentation of this magnificent offering was made on July 2, 1872 A.D. (the hundred and seventy-first anniversary of the Society for the Propagation of the Gospel), in St. Paul's Cathedral. The Bishop of Lichfield (Dr. Selwyn, formerly Bishop of New Zealand) had been commissioned by the American prelates to make the presentation, which he did after reading an address to the archbishops and bishops at home.

The ritual difficulties, which had to some extent been forgotten, or at least withdrawn from popular discussion, by the more exciting and even more bitter controversies regarding the publication of "Essays and Reviews," and the writings of Bishop Colenso, began, in 1866 A.D., to claim once more the general attention of the Church. The "English Church Union" had been founded, in 1859 A.D., to defend the doctrine, discipline, and ritual of the Church, and to afford counsel and protection to all who were prosecuted on such grounds. This society was met by the organizing, in 1865 A.D., of the "Church Association," which was designed "to counteract the efforts now being made to pervert the teaching of the Church of England on essential points of the Christian faith, or assimilate her services to those of the Church of Rome."

In February, 1866 A.D., the archbishop received an important deputation on the subject, and for the next six months the matter was fully debated in Convocation, the final decision arrived at being "that no alteration from the long-sanctioned and usual ritual ought to be made in our Churches until the sanction of the bishop of the diocese has been obtained thereto." This was the first occasion, since its revival in 1852 A.D., on which the provincial synod of Canterbury came to a deliberate resolution upon the ritual controversies which had so long been agitating the Church.

Lord Shaftesbury, whose sympathies were always with the extreme Low Church party, proceeded, on May 14, 1867 A.D., to introduce into the House of Lords his "Clerical Vestments Bill," in spite of the urgent requests of Archbishop Longley, Bishop Tait, and others, that he would postpone his action for a time until the first report of the Royal Commission (which had been promised by the Government) should be published. The primate, "while expressing his full agreement with the greater part of the noble earl's powerful address, and his sympathy with the indignation he had shown, urged the advantage of waiting for the action of the Royal Commission about to be appointed, and moved the postponement of the second reading." The bill was rejected by sixty-one votes to forty-six.

The commissioners, of whom the archbishop was chairman, began their sittings on June 17, and issued their first report on August 19, which was to the effect that the eucharistic vestments are not regarded as essential, and that it is expedient to restrain all innovations in this direction. For a few months the Lambeth Conference diverted the attention of Churchmen from the ritual question. But early in 1868 A.D. the discussions in Convocation were revived, although no decision was arrived at pending the appearance of the second report of the commission.

Archbishop Longley, who was called to his rest before the disestablishment and disendowment of the Irish Church became an accomplished fact, lived long enough to see the commencement of the attack, and to use that influence which he wielded with no slight effect (but in this instance without avail) in the direction of saving the Church in Ireland from spoliation. On March 23, 1868 A.D., Mr. Gladstone proposed his resolutions on the subject. He carried the first division on them by a majority of sixty against the Government, whereupon Mr. Disraeli announced, on May 4, that he had advised her Majesty to dissolve Parliament in the coming autumn, so that the decision of the country might be taken on the Irish Church question. Public meetings on both sides were at once organized in London and in different parts of the country. A gigantic gathering was held at St. James's Hall on May 6, under the presidency of the archbishop, who was supported on the platform by twenty-five bishops (eleven of whom held English sees) and forty-nine peers. His Grace's address at this meeting, and his speech the following month in the three days' debate on the "Suspensory Bill" in the House of Lords, were among his last public utterances.

The venerable archbishop, who was ailing throughout the autumn, died of bronchitis at Addington Park on October 27, 1868 A.D., in the seventy-fifth year of his age.

The following brief *résumé* of the archbishop's life, by one who knew and loved him well, is worth recording: "Charles Thomas Longley, who had been the first bishop of the newly formed see of Ripon, which he held for twenty years, passed in six years through those of Durham and York to that of Canterbury. During his short archiepiscopate of barely six years he evinced a talent for administration, of which he had already given proofs in the lesser sphere of the Ripon diocese, combined with a benignity of disposition which won for him the love and honour of every 'school' and every grade in the English Church. The one event for which his occupancy of the Metropolitical See will be best remembered was the gathering of the first 'Pan-Anglican Conference of Bishops,' an act which, while it marks an epoch in the history of the English Church, is a striking memorial of the profound judgment and true Catholicity of mind for which Archbishop Longley was conspicuous through life. By this act he especially showed how deeply he realized and had the courage to give visible expression to that great spiritual headship of the Anglican Communion which centred in the Metropolitical Chair of Canterbury."

The archbishop was a scholar of no mean order, and a good administrator. While others of more brilliant gifts to some extent eclipsed his fame in public matters, yet the influence of his piety and devotion, and of his unfailing gentleness and chivalrous courtesy, was widely felt, and left its mark upon his generation.

CHAPTER XIV.

ARCHIBALD CAMPBELL TAIT (1868–1882 A.D.).

THE first Scotchman who ever attained to the primacy of the English Church was Archibald Campbell Tait. He was the youngest son of a family of nine, and was born at Harviestoun, in Clackmannanshire, on December 22, 1811 A.D. His mother died when he was only two years old. Shortly afterwards pecuniary trouble fell upon his father, and his childhood was spent in circumstances of privation. At the age of ten he was sent to the High School at Edinburgh, whence in due course he was removed to the newly founded Edinburgh Academy.

After three years spent at Glasgow University, young Tait went up to Balliol, Oxford, in October, 1830 A.D. He had a distinguished career, graduating in 1833 A.D., and in the following year was elected to a Balliol Fellowship. He was ordained in 1836 A.D., and for the next five years he acted as curate in charge of a small country parish nearly six miles from Oxford, discharging his pastoral duties in addition to his college work as tutor and fellow.

At this time the Tractarian movement was in full swing. The celebrated Tract 90, written by Dr. Newman on the interpretation of the Thirty-nine Articles, was issued on February 27, 1841 A.D. A few days later a strong protest, signed by four tutors of Balliol, was published. One of the four was Archibald Tait, among whose papers was found the original draft, identical with the final document except as regards a few verbal differences. Space does not allow of a description of the various phases of the controversy which raged round this question for several years. But the discontinuance of the series of tracts was largely due to the action of Tait and his three co-signatories.

In July, 1842 A.D., he was elected headmaster of Rugby, in succession to Dr. Arnold, and a year later married Catherine, youngest daughter of Archdeacon Spooner. In his school work, as in his University career, he devoted himself heart and soul to the faithful discharge of the duties devolving upon him, but his wonderful zeal and energy gradually overtaxed his strength. In February, 1848 A.D., he was stricken down with rheumatic fever, and within a month the doctors had given up all hope. He gradually recovered, but it was evident that his health had been greatly shaken, and that he would not for a long time, if ever, be equal to a renewal of the tremendous strain of the work done before his illness. Accordingly when, in 1849 A.D., he was offered the deanery of Carlisle, his friends urged him to accept the post.

It is not too much to say that up to that time the universal conception of the decanal office had been one of leisurely and dignified retirement, if not of masterly inactivity. But Tait's six years' tenure of his deanery showed that he, at least, was determined to put forth his full powers in order that he might show himself to be a living force, and not a mere figure-head. A few months after his appointment he was invited to serve on the royal commission "for enquiring into the state, discipline, studies, and revenues of the University of Oxford, and of all and singular the Colleges in the said University." Notwithstanding the vehement opposition which was offered by many of the heads of houses and other academical authorities, the task was persevered in, and a most elaborate and able report was issued, the general tenor of the recommendations being that the doors of the University should be thrown more widely open in various ways.

The two chief items of Dean Tait's reforming work at Carlisle were the reorganization of the capitular revenues, and the restoration of the cathedral.

It was in March and April, 1856 A.D., that the terrible sorrow overwhelmed the occupants of the deanery of Carlisle, when five daughters were carried off by scarlet fever in less than a month, leaving the bereaved parents with two children, a boy aged six, and a baby six weeks old.

A few months later Dean Tait was nominated to the bishopric of London to succeed Bishop Blomfield, who had resigned the see. It is an interesting fact that only once during the previous two hundred years had any man, not already in episcopal orders, been appointed to the diocese of the metropolis.

Dr. Tait was consecrated on November 23, 1856 A.D., in the Chapel Royal, Whitehall, together with Dr. Cotterill (Bishop of Grahamstown, and afterwards Bishop of Edinburgh); and he immediately plunged into the duties of his new sphere of work.

From the very beginning of his career as Bishop of London, he was drawn into the ritual controversies, which for so many years stirred and almost shook to its foundations the Church of England. He sat as an assessor at the Privy Council to hear the appeal of the Hon. and Rev. Robert Liddell, Vicar of St. Paul's, Knightsbridge, against the decision of the Consistory Court of London, and took a prominent part in drawing up the judgment, which was the first of its kind that had been given on the subject of the ornaments of the Church. In his Primary Charge to the diocese, delivered on November 17, 1858 A.D., he dealt at length with the subject of auricular confession, expressing his strong opinion that the inculcation of this as an habitual practice is contrary to the doctrine and custom of the Church of England. The Charge occupied five hours in delivery, and for that space of time he held his hearers, seated under the dome of St. Paul's Cathedral, spell-bound alike by the charm of his manner, and the importance and interest of his utterances. Whether in consequence of this charge, or for other reasons, the "Confession controversy" passed out of sight for many years, until it was revived during his primacy in the year 1873 A.D.

For several years the bishop's tact and skill were severely taxed in dealing with the riots at St. George's-in-the-East, which were fomented and encouraged by the extreme "Protestant" party, and swelled to abnormal proportions by the large element of roughs and criminals abounding in that district.

On the death of Archbishop Sumner in 1862 A.D., and the translation of Dr. Longley from the northern primacy to Canterbury, Bishop Tait was offered the archbishopric of York. After careful consideration, and with the advice of friends, he declined the post on the ground that his duty seemed to lie in the direction of continuing the work of which, during his six years' episcopate, he had so thoroughly mastered the details.

The "Essays and Reviews" controversy has been touched upon in the two preceding memoirs. The position of Bishop Tait, whose friendship with two of the Essayists (Dr. Temple and Professor Jowett) had long been of an intimate character, was necessarily a very difficult one. From the first he urged that the writers should publicly avow their responsibility only for their own productions, and not for the volume as a whole. While maintaining, in Convocation and in his correspondence, the belief that the book was likely to do great and grievous harm, he strongly dissented from the proposal, made after the publication of an episcopal letter, that the Essays should be examined by a committee of the Lower House of Convocation with a view to ascertaining if there were sufficient grounds for a "synodical judgment" to be passed upon them. He was a member of the Judicial Committee of the Privy Council before whom the appeal of two of the Essayists (Dr. Rowland Williams and the Rev. H. B. Wilson), against the condemnation of the Dean of Arches, came, and he joined with the lay judges, in opposition to the two archbishops, in the final judgment which stated that "the charges were not proved." Bearing in mind the fever-heat of popular excitement at the time, and the feeling, which animated a vast number of clergy and laity alike, that the tendency of the volume in question was to undermine the foundations of the Christian faith, it is not surprising that the full tide of wrathful denunciation was turned upon the Bishop of London. Whatever opinion may be held as to the wisdom or the reverse of Bishop Tait's action in the matter, no one will deny that he took a courageous, because a most unpopular, line in accordance with his honest convictions.

In the Colenso controversy also, Dr. Tait, though he had no sympathy with the attack upon Holy Scripture which the Bishop of Natal so gratuitously made in his published works, felt it his duty to oppose the almost unanimous course adopted by his episcopal brethren in inhibiting Dr. Colenso from officiating in their dioceses, and to withstand the strong efforts made by Bishop Wilberforce to secure a formal pronouncement in Convocation that the Church of England was not in communion with Dr. Colenso. His attitude brought him into a position of acute conflict with the fiery Metropolitan of Capetown, but his whole line of policy throughout the controversy, whether the light of after events leads us to believe that he took the wisest course or the reverse, was carefully thought out and planned, and was shaped not merely with reference to the immediate subject in dispute, but rather to the wider question of the relation of the Colonial Churches to the Church at home.

During his London episcopate, Bishop Tait laid himself out, especially in the earlier years of his metropolitan work, to encourage, and even personally to set on foot, a series of evangelistic religious gatherings. He preached at open-air services in almost every part of London; he addressed shiploads of emigrants at the docks, and omnibus-drivers in their great yard at Islington; he preached to the costermongers in Covent Garden market; to railway porters from the platform of a locomotive; to a colony of gipsies on the common of Shepherd's Bush. He managed, after considerable effort and delay, to prevail upon the authorities of Westminster Abbey and St. Paul's Cathedral to hold Sunday evening services, and himself preached on several occasions.

In his Charge to the clergy of the diocese, delivered in 1862 A.D., Bishop Tait described, with many careful statistics, the spiritual destitution of a large number of parishes and districts. He pointed out that three parishes had a population of over thirty thousand, and eleven had upwards of twenty thousand, while there was only one church in each. With the rapid increase of population, amounting to something like forty thousand annually in London alone, the good work done in the matter of church-building (sixty-six permanent, and twenty-one temporary churches had been erected) between the years 1851 and 1861 A.D., had not been able, grand as the effort was, to do more than keep pace with the needs of the time.

Feeling strongly the necessity of endeavouring to cope with the arrears of Church work, and encouraged by the reception accorded to his Visitation Charge, the bishop summoned an influential meeting of the laity, and started the "Bishop of London's Fund," for the strengthening and enlarging of the diocesan work in all its forms. So great was the enthusiasm aroused, that the first subscription list amounted to £60,000, and in March, 1864 A.D., nine months after the appeal was first issued, the total had exceeded £100,000, and £92,000 more had been promised.

When the cholera epidemic broke out in July, 1866 A.D., the Bishop of London was on the point of leaving home for a much-needed rest. But he at once changed his plans, and for many weeks remained, lovingly aided by Mrs. Tait, to minister, both temporarily and spiritually, to the sick and dying. As a sequel to their labours, they established an orphanage at Fulham, which was afterwards moved to St. Peter's, Thanet, where it still exists. The strain, however, had been too great. In September the bishop was taken seriously ill, and for a long time his life hung in the balance. He was able by the following February to resume his active work, although the doctors were constantly urging a relaxation of the severe tension to which he subjected himself by his unceasing efforts.

In the spring of 1868 A.D., he purchased the small estate of Stonehouse, near Broadstairs, as a quiet and bracing retreat, where he could from time to time recuperate his health by a short holiday.

He little thought that before the end of the year he would preside over the see in which this new home was situated.

Archbishop Longley died on October 27, 1868 A.D., and about three weeks later Mr. Disraeli, the then Prime Minister, offered the primacy to Bishop Tait, which he accepted without delay. In less than a fortnight the General Election had taken place, giving a majority of over a hundred to the Opposition, and Mr. Gladstone became the new Premier, pledged to bring forward, as his chief measure, the disestablishment and disendowment of the Irish Church.

It can readily be understood how heavy was the weight of responsibility laid upon the Archbishop of Canterbury, who had only just been raised to this high position, to guide the policy of the Church on the question, and to safeguard the highest religious interests of the nation. In opposing the Suspensory Bill of the previous year, Dr. Tait, who was then Bishop of London, had laid stress on the duty of resisting such a proposal until the feeling of the electorate had been ascertained. The verdict of the nation having now been given with no uncertain voice, the archbishop, contrary to the wishes of a vast number of Churchmen, determined to accept the decision, believing that honesty and consistency required him to do so, and turned his attention to questions of detail, endeavouring to obtain such terms for the Irish Church as would minimize the injustice, and mitigate the severity, of the scheme.

The Bill was introduced by Mr. Gladstone in the

House of Commons on March 1, 1869 A.D.; three weeks later the second reading was carried by a majority of 118; and on May 31 it was read a third time. When it came up to the House of Lords, the Conservative leaders, with a few exceptions, were in favour of summarily rejecting it. The archbishop, however, took a different line. He argued that, in view of the recent judgment of the people, the Bill would be certain to be carried through ultimately, and it would be the wisest course to concentrate all efforts on passing important amendments, after allowing the second reading to be taken. It was largely due to his influence that this plan was adopted. He was in constant communication with the queen, who showed the keenest interest, both in making the best possible terms for the Irish Church, and at the same time in preventing a collision between the two Houses of Parliament. His personal influence with Mr. Gladstone on the one hand, and with the leaders of the Opposition on the other, was exerted, successfully, to bring about a compromise in regard to the amendments proposed, which could be honourably accepted by both contending parties. When the controversy was over, he received warm expressions of thanks from the queen, Mr. Gladstone, and the Irish bishops. Her Majesty assured him of her recognition of his "combined firmness and moderation throughout this unhappy crisis, from the second reading to the end." Archbishop Trench, of Dublin, as representing the Irish prelates, wrote: "All Irish Churchmen, if they are not vulgarly thankless, will keep a most grateful memory of all you did, and sought to do, in aid of our Establishment while it was passing through the crisis of its fate, and I, with those others who were the immediate witnesses of your efforts, will keep the most grateful record of them all."

After the terrible strain, both of responsibility and work, in connection with this Parliamentary struggle, the archbishop spent the late summer in a heavy round of diocesan work. At length, on November 18, 1869 A.D., the overtaxed strength gave way, and he had a convulsive seizure, recurring a few hours later, which left him partially paralyzed on the left side. For many weeks his life was despaired of, and it was not till the following spring that he was able to resume, even tentatively, his active work. Fearing that he might never again be competent to discharge his heavy duties, he desired to resign the primacy, but the queen would not allow him to do this. An alternative plan was finally adopted, by which, under an unrepealed Act of Henry VIII. (26 Henry VIII. cap. 15), he could obtain the assistance of a suffragan bishop, who would relieve him of the greater part of the diocesan work, and thus leave him larger opportunities of dealing with the evergrowing burden of ecclesiastical policy and administration, augmented as it was by the rapidly widening Colonial Church. His choice of suffragan fell on an old Rugby pupil, who had in later years been his domestic chaplain and intimate friend, Archdeacon Edward Parry. Dr. Parry was consecrated Bishop of Dover in Lambeth Palace Chapel on March 25, 1870 A.D., and during his twenty years' episcopate he won, in a marked degree, the affection and esteem of both clergy and laity throughout the diocese of Canterbury.

The storm of opposition roused against the nomination of Dr. Temple to the see of Exeter reached its height during the archbishop's illness, although the objections to the appointment had begun to appear before his seizure. The ground of the complaint was that Dr. Temple had been one of the writers of "Essays and Reviews." Every effort was made, by memorials, by public meetings, at the election by the chapter, and at the confirmation in Bow Church, to prevent Dr. Temple from being raised to the home episcopate. He was, however, consecrated on December 21, 1869 A.D., in Westminster Abbey. Bishop Temple laboured indefatigably in his western diocese for nearly sixteen years, and when, in 1885 A.D., he was translated to the see of London, the appointment was hailed with acclamation by the almost unanimous voice of the Church of England.

We come now to the consideration of a measure which has called forth a vast amount of controversy, and in regard to which the position of Archbishop Tait has been very imperfectly understood. I refer to the Public Worship Regulation Act of 1874 A.D.

For many years Lord Shaftesbury had been exerting himself to alter the constitution and working of the ecclesiastical courts, but his suggestions had met with but feeble support, and the authorities of the Church, in opposing his, as they deemed them, unwise and often mischievous proposals, had pledged themselves to bring in a measure of their own. The bishops met in January, 1874 A.D., to discuss the question, and the two archbishops drafted a Bill, which provided that in every diocese there should be a council, presided over by the bishop, consisting of three incumbents and five lay Churchmen, elected for five years, and three *ex-officio* members. Any complaint of ritual irregularity was to be referred by the bishop to this council, which was to advise him, after hearing evidence, as to whether further proceedings should be taken or not. If the former, the bishop was to issue such order as he deemed necessary, and this was to have the force of law unless annulled by the archbishop on appeal. There was to be no appeal from the archbishop's decision.

Matters, however, were complicated by an unexpected dissolution of Parliament, the defeat of the Liberals at the polls, and the return of the Conservative party with a large majority. Archbishop Tait at once endeavoured to enlist the support of the leading members of the new Government, Mr. Disraeli, Lord Cairns, and Lord Salisbury. But before the Bill could be submitted either to Convocation or to Parliament, the press published an outline of its provisions, and the High Church party, led by Dr. Pusey, vehemently attacked its leading details, especially the diocesan council. At length, on April 20, the archbishop introduced the Bill in the House of Lords. He reluctantly abandoned his proposed council, and fell back on the three assessors (the dean, archdeacon, and a barrister of seven years' standing) provided by the Church Discipline Act of 1840 A.D. The interval between the first and second reading proved, by the criticisms which poured in, that the archbishop could no longer hope for the assistance or support of the High Church party in carrying the legislation that the episcopal bench were unanimous in promoting. When the Bill reached committee, Lord Shaftesbury proposed a series of amendments which, if adopted, must alter the whole character of the measure. The consequence was that the archbishops were placed in the following difficulty. Either they must modify their own wishes as the price of securing the assistance of Lord Shaftesbury and his friends in passing some legislation, or they must abandon the Bill altogether. In the light of after events, it is held by many Churchmen that the latter course would have been the wisest. But, surrounded as the bishops were with a ceaseless chorus of demands for some effort to be made to redress existing grievances, they chose the former alternative. The principal alteration was the transference to a single lay judge, to be appointed by the two archbishops, of the office and authority of the two existing provincial judges, and the provision that all representations under the Act should be heard by this official without the intervention either of diocesan courts, or of the preliminary Commission of Inquiry suggested by the bishops. The most important point of all was the retention, after a severe struggle, of the episcopal veto, which has done much to render comparatively harmless what might otherwise have proved to be a measure disastrous to the Church.

The death of the archbishop's only son, in May,

1878 A.D., followed by that of Mrs. Tait, his beloved and faithful helpmeet and wisest of counsellors, six months later, did much to age him, and to weaken his already enfeebled health.

Perhaps the greatest strain which the primate had to bear during his long episcopate was the task of entering with all his powers into the work of the Second Lambeth Conference, six weeks after the loss of his son. The details of that great gathering are in many respects similar to those of the first conference held under Archbishop Longley. The month of July was given up to the sessions, the second and third weeks being occupied with the work of committees. One hundred and seventy-three bishops (as against one hundred and forty-four in 1867 A.D.) were invited, and one hundred (as against seventy-six) were present.

In the Burials controversy, from 1877 to 1881 A.D., Archbishop Tait was once more placed in a position in which the conscientious discharge of his duty brought him into strong, and to a certain extent bitter, opposition to the views of a large body of the clergy. Whatever opinion may be held as to the line he took, it must be acknowledged that the gloomy foreboding so freely uttered, as to the results of the Burial Act of 1881 A.D., have not been fulfilled. The Act has remained practically a dead letter.

It was to the archbishop's ceaseless efforts, and powerful personal influence, that the Ecclesiastical Courts Commission was appointed, in May, 1881 A.D., with himself as chairman, and, although the report was not issued until after his death, the general tenor was decided upon while he was still presiding over its deliberations.

The principal anxiety of the last few months of his life was to take some steps towards healing the ritual divisions by which the Church was being rent, and he was instrumental in allaying much of the strife and heat of contending parties.

On Advent Sunday, 1882 A.D., after an illness of some three months, Archbishop Tait breathed his last. He was buried in Addington churchyard, in accordance with his own wish, although the offer of a public funeral in Westminster Abbey was made.

The above brief sketch of the part he played in the many difficult crises which arose during his episcopacy will give a fair idea of his character and powers. He is undoubtedly one of the occupants of the see of Canterbury who has earned a high place as in every sense of the word a great man. The Duke of Albany offered the following tribute to his memory: "Archbishop Tait was a high-minded dignitary, an indefatigable worker, a good man; and English history, which records so many heroes of duty, can scarcely point to a purer instance of the single-mindedness which forgets self in great public objects, or of the conscientiousness which makes a man refuse, under any pressure of temptation or weariness, to do less than his utmost, or to be less than his best." A leading statesman, an old pupil of the archbishop's at Rugby, thus described him: "It is not only the Church, it is the State, which may be grateful to the archbishop who conducts the work of his office as Dr. Tait performed his work. I think it may be truly said that he had energy without passion, earnestness without bigotry, and authority without imperiousness."

APPENDIX A.

SUCCESSION OF THE ARCHBISHOPS OF CANTERBURY, FROM THE CONSECRATION OF ST. AUGUSTINE.

With a few exceptions, it may be considered that the date of **the death of an** archbishop is contemporary with the date of the accession **of his successor.**

Names of Archbishops.	Year of Cons. A.D.	Acc. or Trans. A.D.	Names of Archbishops.	Year of Cons. A.D.	Acc. or Trans. A.D.
1 Augustine	597	597	33 Lanfranc	1070	1070
2 Laurentius	604	604	34 Anselm	1093	1093
3 Mellitus	604	619	35 Ralph d'Escures	1108	1114
4 Justus	604	624	36 William de Corbeuil	1123	1123
5 Honorius	627	627	37 Theobald	1139	1139
6 Deusdedit	655	655	38 Thomas à Becket	1162	1162
7 Theodore	668	668	39 Richard	1174	1174
8 Brihtwald	693	693	40 Baldwin	1180	1185
9 Tatwin	731	731	41 Hubert Fitzwalter	1189	1193
10 Nothelm	735	735	42 Stephen Langton	1207	1207
11 Cuthbert	736	741	43 Richard Grant	1229	1229
12 Bregwin	759	759	44 Edmund Rich	1234	1234
13 Jaenbert	766	766	45 Boniface	1245	1245
14 Ethelhard	793	793	46 Robert Kilwardby	1273	1273
15 Wulfred	805	805	47 John Peckham	1279	1279
16 Feologild	832	832	48 Robert Winchelsey	1294	1294
17 Ceolnoth	833	833	49 Walter Reynolds	1308	1313
18 Ethelred	870	870	50 Simon Meopham	1328	1328
19 Plegmund	890	890	51 John Stratford	1323	1333
20 Athelm	909	914	52 Thomas Bradwardine	1349	1349
21 Wulfhelm	914	923	53 Simon Islip	1349	1349
22 Odo	926	942	54 Simon Langham	1366	1366
23 Dunstan	957	960	55 William Whittlesey	1362	1368
24 Ethelgar	980	988	56 Simon Sudbury	1362	1375
25 Siric	985	990	57 William Courtenay	1370	1381
26 Elfric	990	995	58 Thomas Arundel	1374	1397
27 Elphege	984	1005	59 Roger Walden	1398	1398
28 Living	999	1013	60 Henry Chicheley	1408	1414
29 Ethelnoth	1020	1020	61 John Stafford	1425	1443
30 Eadsige	1035	1038	62 John Kemp	1419	1452
31 Robert	1044	1051	63 Thomas Bourchier	1435	1454
32 Stigand (*dep.* 1070)	1043	1052	64 John Morton	1479	1480

APPENDIX.

Names of Archbishops.	Year of Cons. A.D.	Acc. or Trans. A.D.	Names of Archbishops.	Year of Cons. A.D.	Acc. or Trans. A.D.
65 Henry Dean	1496	1501	79 Thomas Tenison	1692	1695
66 William Warham	1502	1503	80 William Wake	1705	1716
67 Thomas Cranmer	1533	1533	81 John Potter	1715	1737
68 Reginald Pole	1556	1556	82 Thomas Herring	1738	1747
69 Matthew Parker	1559	1559	83 Matthew Hutton	1743	1757
70 Edmund Grindal	1559	1576	84 Thomas Secker	1735	1758
71 John Whitgift	1577	1583	85 Frederick Cornwallis	1750	1768
72 Richard Bancroft	1597	1604	86 John Moore	1775	1783
73 George Abbot	1609	1611	87 Charles Manners Sutton	1792	1805
74 William Laud	1621	1633	88 William Howley	1813	1828
75 William Juxon	1633	1660	89 John Bird Sumner	1828	1848
76 Gilbert Sheldon	1660	1663	90 Charles Thos. Longley	1836	1862
77 William Sancroft	1678	1677	91 Archibald Campbell Tait	1856	1868
(*deprived in* 1690)			92 Edward White Benson	1877	1883
78 John Tillotson	1691	1691			

APPENDIX B.

THE ARCHBISHOPS OF CANTERBURY.

(Reprinted by permission from the Canterbury Diocesan Calendar.)

A.D.
- 598. AUGUSTINE, ordained by Etherius, Abp. of Arles; founds Ch. Ch. and St. Augustine's (*c*. 610); buried at St. Augustine's.
- 614. LAURENTIUS, cons. by St. Augustine; reconciles Eadbald to the Church; bur. at St. A.
- 619. MELLITUS, first Bp. of London; bur. at St. A.
- 624. JUSTUS, first Bp. of Rochester; Canterbury confirmed as the metropolitan see by Pope Boniface.
- 627. HONORIUS (cont. with Pope Honorius), cons. by Paulinus, Abp. of York, at Lincoln; bur. at St. A.
- 653. DEUSDEDIT, cons. by Ithamar, Bp. of Rochester; bur. at St. A.
- 666. THEODORE (of Tarsus); councils of Heorford and Hethfield; extends his jurisdiction over all England; arranges dioceses and appoints bishops; bur. at St. A.
- 689. BRIHTWALD, Abbot of Reculver, cons. by Bregwin, Metropol. of Wales— "Up to this time the abps. were sent from Rome, thenceforward they were all Englishmen" (*R. de Diceto, Hist. Archiep. Cant.*); bur. at St. A.
- 726. TATWYNE (death of Bede); bur. at St. A.
- 729. NOTHELM, Pr. of London, cons. at Rome by Pope Gregory II.; bur. at St. A.
- 735. CUTHBERT, Abbot of Lyminge, the first who was buried at Ch. Ch.; all his successors (except Jaenberht) were also buried there.
- 759. BREGWIN; died at Canterbury, bur. at C. C.; called in the obituary "Confessor."
- 763 (or 4). JAENBERHT, Abbot of St. A.; Offa of Mercia endeavours to displace him, but fails.
- 790. ADELARD (or Ethelhard), Bishop of Winchester; obtains a confirmation of the privileges of the see from Pope Leo III. against the King of Mercia.
- 803. WULFRED, cons. at Rome; bur. at C. C.
- 829. FLEODEGILD (or Feologild); dies three months after his election. Vacancy of one year.
- 830. CEOLNOTH; gave Great Chart to C. C.
- 870. ETHELRED, cons. at Rome by Pope Adrian II., sate eighteen years. Vacancy of two years.
- 890 (or 1). PLEGMUND, cons. at Rome by Pope Formosus; holds a council of the West Saxons; ordained seven bps. at C. C.
- 923. ATHELM (or Adhelm); cons. Athelstan K. of England.
- 928. WULFHELM, Bp. of Wells (not mentioned in obituary book).
- 941. ODO (or Otho), Bp. of Malmesbury, called "Confessor" and "the Holy;" cons. Kings Edmund and Edred; removes relics of Wilfrid from Ripon to Canterbury.

APPENDIX.

A.D.

[ALYSNE, Bp of Winchester, who died on his way to Rome, and BRYTHELM, Bp. of Wells, were successively elected, but never sate.]

959. DUNSTAN, Abbot of Glastonbury; cons. Edgar and Edwin the Martyr; was nephew to Abp. Athelm; restores monasticism and incorporates the smaller monasteries with C. C.; bur. at C. C., though his relics were claimed for Glastonbury.

982. ATHELGAR (or Ethelgar), monk of Glastonbury, Abbot of Winchester, Bp. of Selsey; sate only fifteen months.

990. SIRIC (or Siricius), Bp. of Wilton, previously monk of Glastonbury; substitutes regulars for seculars in C. C.

995. ALURIC (or Alfric), Bp. of Wilton, called "Confessor" (Obit.).

1006. ELPHEGE, Prior of Glastonbury, Abbot of Bath, and Bp. of Winchester; murdered by the Danes; bur. at St. Paul's, London; trans. to C. C. by Canute; commemorated as a martyr. Vacancy of a year.

1018. LIVVING, Bp. of Wells; cons. Edmund Ironside and Canute.

1020. ETHELNOTH (or Egelnoth), called the "Good," monk of Glastonbury, Bishop of Lincoln; cons. Harold and Hardicanute.

1038. EADSIN, Harold's chaplain; cons. Edward King of England.

1050. ROBERT, Abbot of Jumièges, Bp. of London; expelled from England as a Norman; bur. at Jumièges.

1052. STIGAND, Harold's chaplain, Bp. of the S. Saxons and afterwards of Winchester; deposed by a council at Winchester; died in prison. Vacancy of two years.

1070. LANFRANC, Abbot of Bec, then of Caen, cons. at Canterbury; asserts the primacy for C. against York; cons. William Rufus; founds St. Alban's Abbey; recovers twenty-one manors for his church; introduces the prebendal instead of the older conventual system; divides the archiep. manors from those of the monastery. Vacancy of four years.

1093. ANSELM, Abbot of Bec, b. at Aosta; controversy on Investiture; forbids marriage of clergy; holds a council in London. Vacancy of five years.

1114. RALPH DE TURBINE, Bp. of Rochester; cons. Adela as Queen of England at Windsor.

1123. WILLIAM CORBOIL, Prior of St. Osyth; cons. Stephen as king contrary to his promise to Queen Matilda; dedicates C. C. in presence of King Henry, May 4, 1130. Vacancy of two years.

1138. THEOBALD, Abbot of Bec; cons. Henry, son of Matilda, as K. of E.

1162. THOMAS À BECKET, Archd. of Canterbury, Provost of Beverley Council of Clarendon; conflict with the king; slain December 22, 1170.

1174. RICHARD, Prior of Dover; C.C. burnt down, 1174; controversy between abp. and Abbot of St. Augustine's closed; dies at Bp. of Rochester's Manor of Halling.

1184. BALDWIN, Bp. of Worcester, made *Legatus natus* by Pope Urban; cons. Richard King of England.; goes to the Holy Land, and dies at Acre. Vacancy of three years.

1193. HUBERT WALTER, Bp. of Salisbury, confirmed in legatine office; cons. King John. Vacancy of three years.

1207. STEPHEN LANGTON, cardinal; England under interdict; **council** at Oxford; monks of C. allowed by the pope to choose their abp.

1229. RICHARD LE GRAND; sate two years. Vacancy of two years.

1233. EDMUND LE RICH, of Abingdon; conflict with King Henry on the Rights of the Church of Canterbury; retires to Pontigny, and dies there; canonized. (The list of Radulphus de Diceto ends here.)

1245. BONIFACE, a Prince of Savoy, uncle to Queen Eleanor; builds the college (or hospital) of Maidstone and the hall of the Palace at Canterbury, Lambeth Chapel; dies at his castle in Savoy.

1272. ROBERT KILWARDBY, of the Order (Dom.) of Friars' Preachers; created cardinal, and takes the sacred vessels and registers of Canterbury to Rome; dies there.

1279. JOHN PECKHAM, a Minorite; urges residence upon the clergy; endeavours to get the restoration of the previous registers; the registers of the see at Lambeth begin with his visitation of his manors in 1279; dies at Mortlake, and is buried at Canterbury in the Martyrdom.

1292. ROBERT DE WINCHELSEY; conflict with King Edward on the Subsidy; exiled, returning, dies at Oxford.

APPENDIX. 207

A.D.
- **1314.** WALTER REYNOLDS ; increase of pluralities ; fall of the Knights Templars ; fresh taxation of abp.'s manors. (The register of Prior Henry de Estria ends here.)
- **1328.** SIMON MEOPHAM ; conflict with the monks of C. C. ; results in his ruin and death, under excommunication, at Mortlake.
- **1333.** JOHN DE STRATFORD ; obtains a reversal of the decree against his predecessor ; forms park at Otford, and endows a college at Stratford-on-Avon, his birthplace.
- **1349.** THOMAS BRADWARDINE ; writes a noble work in defence of the Augustinian doctrine of grace ; dies of the plague a few weeks after his cons. ; Abp. Ufford appointed in his stead, but died before his cons.
- **1349.** SIMON ISLIP ; visits the diocese in 1350 ; prevalence of non-residence of clergy ; pluralities somewhat restricted.
- **1366.** SIMON LANGHAM, cr. cardinal ; increase of pluralities ; rise of Wiclif ; resigns the see.
- **1368.** WILLIAM WHITTLESEY, Bp. of Worcester, nephew of Abp. Islep ; exchanges of livings increase ; Papal Bulls prohibited.
- **1375.** SIMON DE SUDBURY, Bp. of London ; inquires into the state of benefices held by foreigners ; Edward the Black Prince bur. at C. C. ; abp. ordered by the pope to proceed against Wiclif ; great schism of the West, English clergy hold with Urban ; abp. slain in rebellion of Wat Tyler.
- **1381.** WILLIAM COURTENAY, Bp. of Hereford, of London ; builds Saltwood Castle ; persecution of Lollards ; holds a visitation in 1393.
- **1396.** THOMAS ARUNDEL, son of E. of Arundel, by dau. of E. of Lancaster ; attainted, and inventory of his possessions taken at Lyminge ; restored in blood on death of Richard II. ; persecutes the Lollards with the greatest severity ; builds the Arundel Steeple in C. C. and gives five bells to the cathedral ; died at Hackington.
- **1414.** HENRY CHICHELE ; founds All Souls' Coll., Oxford ; founds library of C. C. ; conflict with Card. Beaufort for precedence as *Legatus natus*, ended by Eugenius IV. in favour of the cardinal as *Legatus à latere* ; bur. in C. C. with unusual splendour.
- **1442.** JOHN STAFFORD, Bp. of Bath and Wells ; deaths of Dukes of Exeter and Suffolk, and of Lyndwode, author of the "Provinciale."
- **1452.** JOHN KEMPE, cardinal, of the family of the Kempes of Ollantigh.
- **1454.** THOMAS BOURGCHIER, of the family of the Earls of Ewe ; gives Knole in Sevenoaks to the see ; crowns Edward IV. and celebrates his marriage with Elizabeth Woodville ; cr. cardinal ; entertains king and queen at Canterbury.
- **1486.** JOHN MORTON, a devoted servant of Henry VI. ; restores and increases the buildings of the see at Knole, Maidstone, Aldington, Charing, Ford, Lambeth, and Canterbury ; builds central tower at C. C. and gateway towers at Lambeth ; bur. in C. C., in the crypt.
- **1500.** HENRY DENE (or Deny), dies before his enthronization. (The obituary of C. C. ends here.)
- **1502.** WILLIAM WARHAM, the friend of Erasmus ; visits the diocese in 1511, attended by his chancellor, Cuthbert Tonstal, afterwards Bp. of Durham ; presides at the Convocation which declares the freedom of the C. of E. against the claims of the papacy ; struggles vainly against influence of Wolsey ; bur. in C. C.
- **1533.** THOMAS CRANMER ; opening of Reformation ; dissolution of monasteries ; compilation of Liturgy and Articles ; breach with the papacy ; Convocation, originally employed for civil purposes, assumes the form of a synod, and a legislative position in the Church ; abp. deprived by Q. Mary, and executed.
- **1556.** REGINALD POLE, cardinal ; "reconciliation" of England with the papacy ; visitation of diocese discloses the ruin and desolation of the churches, and the loss or destruction of their furniture and vestments ; the cardinal dies on the same day as the queen ; buried hastily under a temporary brick grave in C. C., over which were his arms and quarterings, now obliterated.
- **1559.** MATTHEW PARKER, chaplain to Q. Anne Boleyn ; Reformation re-established ; Liturgy of 1562 substituted for that of 1552 ; rise of the Puritans ; abp. visits the diocese in 1561 and 1571 ; bur. at Lambeth.
- **1575.** EDMUND GRINDAL, endeavours to reconcile the Puritans by encouraging

APPENDIX.

A.D.

meetings for prayer and exposition of Scriptures; offends the queen and the High Ch. party; praised by the learned continental Reformers.

1583. JOHN WHITGIFT, Calvinist in doctrine, but affecting the princely habits of the most worldly of his predecessors; frames the "Lambeth Articles;" recovers the property of the see; and endows churches out of the money thus acquired; assists at the Hampton Court Conf.

1604. RICHARD BANCROFT; opposes Calvinism and the Scotch and Genevan discipline; assists at the Hampton Court Conference as Bp. of London; admired by Clarendon.

1610. GEORGE ABBOTT; reaction in favour of Puritanism; neglect of churches, and adoption of Genevan forms; abp. popular with the Puritan party, but by his great laxity prepares the way for the troubles which succeeded his episcopate.

1633. WILLIAM LAUD; conflict opens in the diocese; Kentish petition invokes the aid of Parliament against the bps.; Sir Edward Dering's "Committee on Religion," 1641; outbreak of the Rebellion, in which the king and the abp. perish. Abp. Laud was martyred in 1645. *Interregnum* of the archbishopric till the Restoration.

1660. WILLIAM JUXON, the companion of Charles I. on the scaffold; conciliates the Nonconformists.

1663. GILBERT SHELDON, a violent enemy of the Puritans; urges the putting into execution of all the laws against Nonconformity; chief promoter of the Act of Uniformity and of the "Five-mile Act;" renders the schism incurable; is a munificent benefactor of the U. of Oxford.

1677. WILLIAM SANCROFT (or Sandcroft); resists the attempts of James II. to introduce popery by the way of ";Toleration;" one of the "Petitioners" sent to the Tower; refuses after the Revolution to take the oath of allegiance to William and Mary; deprived of the archbishopric; retires to his estate of Fressingfield in Suffolk, and dies there.

1691. JOHN TILLOTSON; Sancroft continues his refusal to take the oath to W. and M. and is deposed; secession of the Nonjurors; Revolution vindicated by Bp. Lloyd; publication of Overall's Convocation Book by Sancroft; Toleration Act passed; abp. dies one year after Sancroft.

1695. THOMAS TENISON; promotes toleration; controversy on "Occasional Conformity;" founds chapel and library for St. Martin's-in-the-Fields; preaches funeral sermon on Q. Mary.

1715. WILLIAM WAKE; engages in controversy with Bossuet in earlier life; efforts at reunion with Rome by means of mutual concession; restores palaces at Lambeth and Croydon; leaves large bequests to Ch. Ch., Oxford.

1736. JOHN POTTER; recognizes Moravian Brethren as an ancient Episcopal Church and Count Zinzendorf as bishop; promotes union of Nonconformists; a learned abp. and zealous diocesan; Wesley preaches in Kent, 1738.

1747. THOMAS HERRING; restores palace of Croydon; rise of Methodism; it spreads rapidly over Kent; opening of the darkest period of C. of E., which extends over the next five primacies.

1757. MATTHEW HUTTON, never resided at Lambeth; bur. at Lambeth Church. He was descended from Dr. Matthew Hutton, Abp. of York in Q. Elizabeth's reign.

1758. THOMAS SECKER, a popular writer of sermons, originally studied medicine; Bp. of Oxford for twenty years; assisted in establishing American bishoprics; a munificent benefactor of the Church societies; Dr. Porteus, Bp. of London, was among his chaplains, as he was of his successor, Abp. Cornwallis.

1768. FREDERICK CORNWALLIS, of the family of the Marquis Cornwallis, lived in great state at Lambeth; little known in the diocese; attack of Lambeth Palace during riots of 1780.

1783. JOHN MOORE; period of the great sinecures and of nepotism in the Church; spread of Methodism in Kent. During this primacy were consecrated Samuel Seabury at Aberdeen to be Bp. of Connecticut, and first bp. of the American Church, on Nov. 14, 1784; and the following in Lambeth Palace Chapel—viz. the second, third, and fourth bps. of the American Church, William White, Pennsylvania, and Samuel Provoost, New York,

A.D.	
	on Feb. 4, 1787; James Madison, Virginia, Sept. 19, 1790; the first of the Colonial bishops, Charles Inglis, Nova Scotia, Aug. 12, 1787; and Jacob Mountain, Quebec, July 7, 1793.
1805.	CHARLES MANNERS SUTTON, of the ducal family of Rutland; carries on the traditions of his two immediate predecessors; always visits the diocese in state; age of pluralities and continued nepotism; Addington purchased for the see.
1828.	WILLIAM HOWLEY, Bp. of London; crowns William IV. and Queen Adelaide and Queen Victoria; Eccl. Commission created; changes in the episcopate; last Abp. under the earlier system; bur. at Addington.
1848.	JOHN BIRD SUMNER, Bp. of Chester; controversies arising out of the Oxford Movement, Essays and Reviews, Bp. Colenso's publications; Gorham appeal, difference between Abp. and Bp. of Exeter thereupon, fulfils all diocesan duties to an advanced age; bur. at Addington.
1862.	CHARLES THOMAS LONGLEY, first Bp. of Ripon, then Bp. of Durham, then Abp. of York, then elevated to Canterbury; Gen. Conference of Anglican bps. at Lambeth; institutes Church Building and Endowment Society for the diocese; bur. at Addington.
1868.	ARCHIBALD CAMPBELL TAIT, Dean of Carlisle, Bp. of London; second Conference of Anglican bps. at Lambeth; presides over the Commissions for Cathedral Reform and Eccl. Courts Inquiry; bur. at Addington.

APPENDIX C.

List of Archbishops of Canterbury mentioned in this Volume, with Date of Consecration, and the Bishops they consecrated.

(Taken from Stubbs' "Episcopal Succession in England," as far as the year 1857, and subsequently from the official Registers of the Archbishop of Canterbury.)

Name.	When and where consecrated.	By whom consecrated.	Bishops consecrated by him.	
AUGUSTINE	Nov. 16, 597, at Arles	Vergilius	Mellitus (London)	604
			Justus (Rochester)	604
			Laurentius (Canterbury)	604
THEODORE	Mar. 26, 668, at Rome	Pope Vitalian	Putta (Rochester)	669
			Bisa (Dunwich)	669
			Leutherius (Dorchester)	670
			Winfrid (Lichfield)	672
			Bedwin (Elmham)	673
			Etti (Dunwich)	673
			Saxulf (Lichfield)	675
			Erkenwald (London)	675
			Cuichelm (Rochester)	676
			Headda (Winchester)	676
			Bosa (York)	678
			Gebmund (Rochester)	678
			Bosel (Worcester)	680
			Cuthwin (Leicester)	680
			Ethelwin (Lindsey)	680
			Trumwin (Whithern)	681
			Trumbert (Hexham)	681
			Cuthbert (Lindisfarne)	685
			John (Hexham)	687
ANSELM	Dec. 4, 1093, at Canterbury	Thomas of York	Bloett (Lincoln)	1094
		Maurice of London	Saml o' Haingley (Dublin)	1096
		Walkelin of Winchester	Gerard (Hereford)	1096
			Samson (Worcester)	1096
			Malchus (Waterford)	1096
		Gundulf of Rochester	Wm. Giffard (Winchester)	1107
			Roger (Salisbury)	1107
		Osmund of Salisbury	Wm. Warelwast (Exeter)	1107
			Reinhelm (Hereford)	1107
		Robert of Hereford	Urban (Llandaff)	1107
			Richd. de Beames (London)	1108
		Robert of Lichfield	Ralph d'Escures (Rochester)	1108

APPENDIX.   211

Name.	When and where consecrated.	By whom consecrated.	Bishops consecrated by him.
ANSELM (*continued*)		John of Bath Ralph of Chichester Herbert of Thetford	
BECKET	June 3, 1162, at Canterbury	Henry of Winchester Nigel of Ely Robert of Bath Jocelin of Sarum William of Norwich Hilary of Chichester Walter of Rochester Nicolas of Llandaff Gilbert of Hereford Robert of Lincoln David of St. David's Geoffrey of St. Asaph Richard of Lichfield Bartholomew of Exeter	Robert of Maledon (Hereford) ... ... 1163 Roger Fitz Count (Worcester) 1164
CHICHELEY	June 17, 1408, at Lucca (St. David's).	Pope Gregory XII.	Stephen Patrington (St. David's) ... ... 1415 John Wakering (Norwich) 1416 Edmund Lacy (Hereford) 1417 John Chandler (Salisbury) 1417 John Langdon (Rochester) 1422 Wm. Gray (London) ... 1426 John Rickingale (Chichester) 1426 William Alnwick (Norwich) 1426 Robert Neville (Salisbury) 1427 Thomas Brown (Rochester) 1435 William Wells (Rochester) 1437 Richard Praty (Chichester) 1438
WARHAM	Sept. 25, 1502, at Fulham (London)	Richard of Winchester John of Exeter	David ap Owen (St. Asaph) 1504 Richard Mayew (Hereford) 1504 William Barons (London) 1504 John Fisher (Rochester) ... 1504 Hugh Oldham (Exeter) ... 1505 Robt. Sherborn (St. David's) 1505 John Penny (Bangor) ... 1505 James Stanley (Ely) ... 1506 Thos Skirvington (Bangor) 1509 Edmund Birkhead (S. Asaph) 1513 Thomas Wolsey (Lincoln) 1514 William Atwater (Lincoln) 1514

APPENDIX.

Name.	When and where consecrated.	By whom consecrated.	Bishops consecrated by him.
WARHAM (*continued*)			Nicolas West (Ely) 1515 Charles Booth (Hereford) 1516 Henry Standish (St. Asaph) 1518 John Voysey (Exeter) 1519 John Longlands (Lincoln) 1521 Cuthbert Tonstall (London) 1522 Richd. Rawlins (St. David's) 1523
CRANMER	Mar. 30, 1533, at Westminster	John of Lincoln John of Exeter Henry of St. Asaph	Thomas Goodrich (Ely) 1534 Rowland Lee (Lichfield) 1534 John Salcot (Bangor) 1534 Nicolas Shaxton (Salisbury) 1535 Edward Fox (Hereford) 1535 Hugh Latimer (Worcester) 1535 John Hilsey (Rochester) 1535 George Brown (Dublin) 1536 Thomas Manning (Ipswich) 1536 John Salisbury (Thetford) 1536 Richd. Sampson (Chichester) 1536 William Barlow (St. David's) 1536 William Rugg (Norwich) 1536 Robert Parfew (St. Asaph) 1536 Lewis Thomas (Shrewsbury) 1537 John Bird (Penreth) 1537 Thos. Morley (Marlborough) 1537 John Bell (Worcester) 1539 John Skip (Hereford) 1539 John Wakeman (Gloucester) 1541 George Day (Chichester) 1543 Robert Ferrar (St. David's) 1548 John Poynet (Rochester) 1550 John Hooper (Gloucester) 1551 Miles Coverdale (Exeter) 1551 John Scory (Rochester) 1551 John Taylor (Lincoln) 1552 John Harley (Hereford) 1553
PARKER	Dec. 17, 1559, at Lambeth	William of Chichester John of Hereford John of Bedford Miles (*ex*) of Exeter	Edmund Grindal (London) 1559 Richard Cox (Ely) 1559 Rowland Meyrick (Bangor) 1559 Edwyn Sandys (Worcester) 1559 Nicolas Bullingham (Lincoln) 1560 John Jewell (Salisbury) 1560 Thomas Young (St. David's) 1560 Richard Davies (St. Asaph) 1560 Edmund Gheast (Rochester) 1560 Gilbert Berkeley (Bath) 1560 Thomas Bentham (Coventry) 1560 William Alley (Exeter) 1560 John Parkhurst (Norwich) 1560 Robert Horne (Winchester) 1561 Edmund Scambler (Peterborough) 1561 Thomas Davis (St. Asaph) 1561 Richd. Cheyney (Gloucester) 1562 Hugh Jones (Llandaff) 1566 Nicolas Robinson (Bangor) 1566 Richard Rogers (Dover) 1569

APPENDIX.

Name.	When and where consecrated.	By whom consecrated.	Bishops consecrated by him.
PARKER (*continued*)			Richard Curteis (Chichester) 1570 Thomas Cowper (Lincoln) 1571 William Bradbridge (Exeter) 1571 Edmund Freke (Rochester) 1572 William Hughes (St. Asaph) 1573 William Blethin (Llandaff) 1575
LAUD	Nov. 18, 1621, at London House (St. David's)	George of London John of Worcester Nicolas of Ely George of Chichester John of Oxford Theophilus of Llandaff	William Juxon (London) ... 1633 Edmund Griffith (Bangor) 1634 Francis Dee (Peterborough) 1634 Matthew Wren (Hereford) 1635 Roger Mainwaring (St. David's) ... ... 1636 Robert Skinner (Bristol) ... 1637 William Roberts (Bangor) 1637 John Warner (Rochester)... 1638 Brian Duppa (Chichester) 1638 John Towers (Peterborough) 1639 Morgan Owen (Llandaff)... 1640
SANCROFT	Jan. 27, 1678, at Westminster	Henry of London Seth of Salisbury Joseph of Peterborough John of Rochester Peter of Ely Guy of Bristol Thomas of Lincoln Thomas of Exeter	William Gulston (Bristol) 1679 William Beaw (Llandaff)... 1679 William Lloyd (St. Asaph) 1680 Robt. Frampton (Gloucester) 1681 Francis Turner (Rochester) 1683 Lawrence Womock (St. David's) ... ... 1683 Thomas Spratt (Rochester) 1684 Thomas Ken (Bath) ... 1685 Baptist Levinz (Sodor and Man) ... ... 1685 Thos. White (Peterborough) 1685 Jonathan Trelawney (Bristol) 1685 John Lloyd (St. David's)... 1685 Samuel Parker (Oxford) ... 1686 Thos. Cartwright (Chester) 1686 Thos. Watson (St. David's) 1687 Timothy Hall (Oxford) ... 1688
HOWLEY	Oct. 3, 1813, at Lambeth (London)	Charles of Canterbury George J. of Gloucester John of Salisbury William of Oxford	John Matthew Turner (Calcutta) ... ... 1829 Richard Bagot (Oxford) ... 1829 James Henry Monk (Gloucester) ... ... 1830 Henry Philpotts (Exeter) 1831 Edward Maltby (Chichester) 1831 Daniel Wilson (Calcutta)... 1832 Edward Grey (Hereford)... 1832 Joseph Allen (Bristol) ... 1834 Daniel Corrie (Madras) ... 1835 Geo. Jeh. Mountain (Montreal) ... ... 1836 Wm. G. Broughton (Australia) ... ... 1836 Samuel Butler (Lichfield) 1836 William Otter (Chichester) 1836 Edward Denison (Salisbury) 1837 Edward Stanley (Norwich) 1837

APPENDIX.

Name.	When and where consecrated.	By whom consecrated.	Bishops consecrated by him.
HOWLEY (*continued*)			Thos. Musgrave (Hereford) 1837
			Thomas Carr (Bombay) ... 1837
			Geo. John T. Spencer (Madras) 1837
			James Bowstead (Sodor and Man) 1838
			George Davys (Peterboro') 1839
			Aubrey Geo. Spencer (Newfoundland) 1839
			John Strachan (Toronto) ... 1839
			Connop Thirlwall (St. David's) 1840
			P. N. Shuttleworth (Chichester) 1840
			George Augustus Selwyn (New Zealand) 1841
			Mich. Solomon Alexander (Jerusalem) 1841
			Ash. Turner Gilbert (Chichester) 1842
			John Lonsdale (Lichfield) 1843
			Ed. Field (Newfoundland) 1844
			Thomas Turton (Ely) ... 1845
			John Medley (Fredericton) 1845
			John Chapman (Colombo) 1845
			Saml. Wilberforce (Oxford) 1845
			Samuel Gobat (Jerusalem) 1846
			Robert Gray (Capetown) 1847
			Augustus Short (Adelaide) 1847
			Charles Perry (Melbourne) 1847
			William Tyrrell (Newcastle) 1847
SUMNER	Sept. 14, 1828, at York (Chester)	Edward of York Charles Richard of Winchester Christopher of Gloucester	Renn Dick Hampden (Hereford) 1848
			George Smith (Victoria) ... 1849
			David Anderson (Rupert's Land) 1849
			Samuel Hinds (Norwich)... 1849
			Alfred Ollivant (Llandaff) 1849
			Thomas Dealtry (Madras) 1849
			Francis Fulford (Montreal) 1850
			Hibbert Binney (Nova Scotia) 1851
			John Harding (Bombay) ... 1851
			Owen E. Vidal (Sierra Leone) 1852
			John Jackson (Lincoln) ... 1853
			John Armstrong (Grahamstown) 1853
			John Wm. Colenso (Natal) 1853
			Walter Kerr Hamilton (Salisbury) 1854
			Francis Barker (Sydney) 1854
			Vincent William Ryan (Mauritius) 1854
			John Wills Weeks (Sierra Leone) 1855
			Reginald Courtenay (Jamaica) 1856

APPENDIX. 215

Name.	When and where consecrated.	By whom consecrated.	Bishops consecrated by him.
SUMNER (*continued*)			Charles Baring (Gloucester and Bristol) ... 1856
			Henry J. C. Harper (Christ Church, N. Z.) ... 1856
			Archibald Campbell Tait (London) ... 1856
			Henry Cotterill (Grahamstown) ... 1856
			John Thomas Pelham (Norwich) ... 1857
			Matthew Blagden Hale (Perth) ... 1857
			John Bowen (Sierra Leone) 1857
			Benjamin Cronyn (Huron) 1857
			Stephen Jordan Rigand (Antigua) ... 1858
			George Ed. Lynch Cotton (Calcutta) ... 1858
			Edmund Hobhouse (Nelson, N. Z.) ... 1858
			Charles John Abraham (Wellington, N. Z.) ... 1858
			George Hills (British Columbia) ... 1859
			James Colquhoun Campbell (Bangor) ... 1859
			Piers Calverley Claughton (St. Helena) ... 1859
			Edward Wyndham Tufnell (Brisbane) ... 1859
			Edward Hyndman Beckles (Sierra Leone) ... 1860
			Joseph Cotton Wigram (Rochester) ... 1860
			William Walrond Jackson (Antigua) ... 1860
			Henry Philpott (Worcester) 1861
			Frederick Gell (Madras) ... 1861
			Charles Caulfield (Nassau) 1861
			William Thomson (Gloucester and Bristol) ... 1861
			Thomas Nettleship Staley (Hawaii) ... 1861
LONGLEY	Nov. 6, 1836, at York (Ripon)	Edward of York John of Lincoln Hugh of Carlisle John Bird of Chester	William George Tozer (Nyassa) ... 1863
			Edward Twells (Orange River) ... 1863
			Charles John Ellicott (Gloucester and Bristol) ... 1863
			Mesac Thomas (Goulburn) 1863
			Addington R. P. Venables (Nassau) ... 1863
			Edward Harold Browne (Ely) ... 1864
			Francis Jeune (Peterboro') 1864
			Charles Henry Bromby (Tasmania) ... 1864

APPENDIX.

Name.	When and where consecrated.	By whom consecrated.	Bishops consecrated by him.	
LONGLEY (*continued*)			Samuel Adjai Crowther (West Africa)	1864
			Robert Machray (Rupert's Land)	1865
			Henry Lascelles Jenner (Dunedin, N. Z.)	1866
			Andrew Burn Suter (Nelson, N. Z.)	1866
			Robert Milman (Calcutta)	1867
			Charles Richard Alford (Victoria)	1867
			William Collinson Sawyer (New South Wales)	1867
			Thomas Legh Claughton (Rochester)	1867
			James B. K. Kelly (Newfoundland)	1867
			Charles Amyand Harris (Gibraltar)	1868
			James Atlay (Hereford)	1868
TAIT	Nov. 23, 1856, at Whitehall (London).	John Bird of Canterbury Ash. Turner of Chichester John of Lincoln Henry M. of Carlisle Aubrey Geo. of Jamaica David of Rupert's Land	Henry Alexander Douglas (Bombay)	1869
			Christopher Wordsworth (Lincoln)	1869
			Thomas Goodwin Hatchard (Mauritius)	1869
			James Francis Turner (Grafton and Armidale)	1869
			William Garden Cowie (Auckland, N. Z.)	1869
			Samuel Edward Marsden (Bathurst)	1869
			Walter Chambers (Labuan)	1869
			Ashton Oxenden (Montreal)	1869
			George Moberly (Salisbury)	1869
			Hugh Willoughby Jermyn (Colombo)	1871
			Alfred Willis (Hawaii)	1872
			Peter Sorensen Royston (Mauritius)	1872
			John Horden (Moosonee)	1872
			William Armstrong Russell (North China)	1872
			John Mitchinson (Barbadoes)	1873
			James Russell Woodford (Ely)	1873
			Charles Waldegrave Sandford (Gibraltar)	1874
			William Carpenter Bompas (Athabasca)	1874
			John M'Lean (Saskatchewan)	1874
			William West Jones (Capetown)	1874
			William Basil Jones (St. David's)	1874

APPENDIX. 217

Name.	When and where consecrated.	By whom consecrated.	Bishops consecrated by him.	
TAIT (*continued*)			Edward Steere (Central Africa)	1874
			Samuel Thornton (Ballarat)	1875
			Reginald Stephen Copleston (Colombo)	1875
			Louis George Mylne (Bombay)	1876
			James Moorhouse (Melbourne)	1876
			Edward Ralph Johnson (Calcutta)	1876
			Edward White Benson (Truro)	1877
			Anthony Wilson Thorold (Rochester)	1877
			Thomas Valpy French (Lahore)	1877
			Jonathan Holt Titcomb (Rangoon)	1877
			Edward Trollope (Nottingham)	1877
			Henry Brougham Bousfield (Pretoria)	1878
			Llewellyn Jones (Newfoundland)	1878
			F. A. R. Cramer Roberts (Nassau)	1878
			George Henry Stanton (North Queensland)	1878
			William Dalrymple Maclagan (Lichfield)	1878
			William Ridley (Caledonia)	1879
			John M. Speechly (Travancore)	1879
			William Walsham How (Bedford)	1879
			Joseph Barclay (Jerusalem)	1879
			Aston Windeyer Sillitoe (New Westminster)	1879
			Josiah Brown Pearson (Newcastle, N. S. W.)	1880
			Enos Nuttall (Jamaica)	1880
			Charles Perry Scott (North China)	1880
			George Evans Moule (North China)	1880
			George Frederick Hose (Singapore and Labuan)	1881
			John Miller Strachan (Rangoon)	1882
			Herbert Bree (Barbadoes)	1882
			Alfred Blomfield (Colchester)	1882
			Charles James Branch (Coadjutor, Antigua)	1882

[NOTE.—*The above list gives the names of those Bishops only who were actually consecrated by the respective Archbishops, and does not include the names of those consecrated under a commission from the Archbishop.*]

INDEX.

A.

	PAGE
Abbot, Archbishop of Canterbury	114
Advertisements, Parker's	110
Agatho, Pope	26
Aidan, St.	20
Albany, Duke of	201
Alexander, Bishop in Jerusalem	148
Alexander, Pope	58
All Souls' College, Oxford	73
America, Church in	153
Andrewes, Bishop of Winchester	117
Anselm, Archbishop of Canterbury	**34-47**
Arches, Court of	132, 150, 165, 173
Ariminum, Council of	8
Arles, Council of	8
Arnold, Dr.	187
Arthur, Prince	81, 90
Articles, The Six	96
——, The Ten	98
——, The Thirteen	109
——, The Thirty-nine	109, 111
——, The Forty-two	109
Arundel, Archbishop of Canterbury	66
Association of Friends of the Church	144
Augustine, Archbishop of Canterbury	**7-19**
Augustine's Oak, Conference at	17

B.

Baden Powell, Professor	165
Bancroft, Archbishop of Canterbury	114
Barclay, Bishop in Jerusalem	148
Barlow, Bishop of Bath and Wells	106
Bate, Rev. George	127
Becket, Archbishop of Canterbury	**48-61, 96**
Benedict Biscop	22
Bertha, Queen of Kent	11
Bible, English version of	97, 109
Bill for Union	139
Bishop of London's Fund	193

	PAGE
Bishops, Appointment of	63
Bishops' Book, The	98
Blomfield, Bishop of London	146, 155, 188
Boleyn, Anne	91, 95, 101
Brooks, Bishop of Gloucester	100
Buckingham, Duke of	117
Burials Controversy	200
Burnet, Bishop of Salisbury	139
Butler, Charles	107

C.

Cairns, Lord	198
Calvinists	79, 103, 115
Canterbury Cathedral	14
——, St. Augustine's College	14
Carmelites	65
Cave-Browne, Rev. J.	159
Cecil	105
Celibacy of the clergy	96, 103
Chad, Bishop of York	24, 33
Chalcedon, Council of	27
Charles I.	114, 126
Charles II.	128, 131
Chicheley, Archbishop of Canterbury	**62-75**
Church Association	182
—— Building	157
—— Discipline Act	198
—— Missionary Society	147
Clarendon, Constitutions of	55
Clerical Vestments Bill	182
Cloveshoo, Council of	28, 34
Codex E	30
Colenso, Bishop	168, 175, 180, 191
Colet, Dean	76
Colonial Bishoprics Fund	146
Colonial Episcopate, Growth of	152
Columba, St.	8
"Confession" Controversy	189
Congé d'élire	63, 92, 106
Consistory Courts	132
Convocation	85, 93, 123, 140, 167, 174
——, revival of	163

INDEX.

Cotterill, Bishop of Grahamstown 189
Coverdale, Miles 107
Cranmer, Archbishop of Canterbury ... 89-100
Cromwell, Oliver 127
Crumwell, Thomas 92, 96

D.

Dean, Archbishop of Canterbury ... 81
Dean of Chapels Royal ... 117
Declaration for liberty of conscience 133
—— of abhorrence 137
Deusdedit, Archbishop of Canterbury 21
Directory of Public Worship ... 126
Discipline, Church 146
Disraeli, Mr. 183, 198
Dissenters 133, 140, 144
Divorce of Queen Katharine ... 94
Doane, Bishop of New Jersey ... 132
Dominicans 65

E.

Easter, Date of observance... 17, 21, 27
Ebbsfleet, landing of St. Augustine at 11
Ecclesiastical Commission 142, 156, 171
—— Courts Commission ... 200
Education, Elementary ... 150
Elizabeth, Queen ... 101, 105, 113
Emancipation (Roman Catholic) Act 142
English Church Union ... 182
Episcopate, Increase of ... 24, 171
Erasmus 76, 83
Erastianism 140
"Essays and Reviews" 165, 173, 181, 190
Ethelbert, King of Kent ... 11
——, Conversion of 14
Evangelicals 159, 169
Evelyn, John 127, 129

F.

Fire of London 130
Fisher, Controversy with Laud ... 115
Fox, Bishop of Hereford ... 90
Franciscans 65
Fulford, Bishop of Montreal ... 180
Fulham Orphanage 193
—— Palace 151

G.

Gardyner, Bishop of Winchester ... 89
George I. 140

George IV. 143
Gladstone, Mr. ... 146, 183, 194
Gobat, Bishop in Jerusalem ... 148
Golden Rose 83
Goodwin, Mr. C. W. 166
Gorham, Rev. G. C., controversy 149, 160
Gray, Bishop of Capetown 168, 171, 196
Gregory the Great, Pope ... 9, 11, 15
Gregory VII., Pope 45
Gregory XI., Pope 67
Gregory XII., Pope 67
Grindal, Archbishop of Canterbury 113
Grossetête, Bishop of Lincoln ... 63

H.

Hadleigh Conference 144
Hadrian, monk 21, 29
Hampden, Dr. 149
Harrow School 170
Hatfield, Synod of 28
Henry VII. 82
Henry VIII. 82, 90
Hertford, Council of ... 27
High Commission, Court of 118, 132, 136
Hodgkins, Bishop of Bedford ... 107
Homilies 98
Hopkins, Bishop of Vermont ... 180
Howley, Archbishop of Canterbury ... 139-153
Hugh, Bishop of Lincoln ... 63

I.

Innocent VII., Pope 66
Ireland 121
Irish Church, Disestablishment of 183, 19

J.

James I. 114, 116
James II. 131
Jerusalem, Bishopric in ... 147
Jewel's "Apology" 108
John's, St., College, Oxford ... 73
Jowett, Professor ... 166, 190
Judicial Committee of Privy Council 173, 190
Justus, Bishop of Rochester ... 15
Juxon, Archbishop of Canterbury 121, 128

K.

Katharine, Queen ... 81, 90, 94
Ken, Bishop of Bath and Wells ... 134

INDEX.

L.

	PAGE
Lambeth Conference	177, 200
—— Palace	74, 106, 112, 120, 134, 145, 179
Lanfranc, Archbishop of Canterbury	36
Latimer	99
Latitudinarianism	128, 140
Laud, Archbishop of Canterbury	**113-125**
Laurentius, Archbishop of Canterbury	20
Lay work	157
Learning, Revival of	78
Leicester, Earl of	109
Liddell, Hon. and Rev. R.	165, 189
Lingard	107
Litany in English	98
Liturgy for Anglican Church	15
Lollard's Tower, Lambeth Palace	73
Longley, Archbishop of Canterbury	**170-185**
Long Parliament	123
Luidhard, Bishop of Senlis	12
Lutherans	79, 103

M.

Magna Charta	63
Manchester, Diocese of	171
Martin, St., Roman Church of	12
Martin V., Pope	71
Mary, Queen	99
Maurice, Rev. F. D.	148
Mellitus, Bishop of London	15
Methodism	140, 157
Monasteries inspected	22
—— suppressed	64
Monmouth's rebellion	132
Montagu, Dr.	116
More, Sir Thomas	77, 83, 87
Mortmain, Statute of	64
Musgrave, Archbishop of York	173

N.

"Nag's Head Fable"	107
National Society	150
Neile, Bishop of Winchester	117
Newman, Rev. John Henry	148
Ninian, St.	8
Non-jurors	138
Non-residence Act	146
Northampton, Council of	56

O.

Oates, Titus	130
Offa, King of Mercia	35
Oldcastle, Sir John	69

P.

	PAGE
Papal claims, Resistance to	26, 35, 48, 75, 93
Parker, Archbishop of Canterbury	**101-112**
Parochial system, origin of	23
Parr, Katharine	102
Parry, Bishop of Dover	196
Paschal, Pope	46
Patrick, St.	8
Pattison, Rev. Mark	166
Paul IV., Pope	105
Paulinus, Archbishop of York	15, 20
Penitentiary of England	92
Petition of Right	117
Philpotts, Bishop of Exeter	158, 161
Pius V., Pope	110
Pluralities Act	146
Pole, Cardinal	106
Præmunire, Statute of	64, 72
Prayer-book	99, 103
Presbyterianism	126, 139
Protestants	103
Provisors, Statute of	64
Public Worship Regulation Act	197
Puritans	103, 114, 124
Pusey, Dr.	198

R.

Reformation	79, 94, 103
Reform Bill	142, 158
Ridley	99
Ripon, Diocese of	171
Ritual disputes	165, 189
Roman hierarchy in England	111, 164
Rose, Rev. Hugh James	144
Rye House Plot	131

S.

Salisbury, Marquis of	198
Sancroft, Archbishop of Canterbury	**126-138**
Sardica, Council of	8
Savoy Conference	128
Scory, Bishop of Rochester	107
Selwyn, Bishop of Lichfield	181
Shaftesbury, Earl of	182, 197
Sheldon, Archbishop of Canterbury	128
Short Parliament	122
Society for Promoting Christian Knowledge	147
Society for Propagation of Gospel	147, 181
Solemn League and Covenant	122, 128
Star Chamber	118
Stigand, Archbishop of Canterbury	36
Stonehouse, Kent	193
Strafford, Earl of	120, 123
Streanæshale, Synod of	21
Suffragan Bishops	196

INDEX

S (cont.)

Sumner, Archbishop of Canterbury ... 154–169
Sumner, Bishop of Winchester ... 156
Supremacy, Royal ... 77, 87, 106

T.

Tait, Archbishop of Canterbury ... 186–202
Temple, Bishop of Exeter 165, 190, 197
Test Act ... 131
Theobald, Archbishop of Canterbury ... 42
Theodore, Archbishop of Canterbury ... 20–33
Thirlwall, Bishop of St. David's ... 179
Tierney, Canon ... 107
Tillotson, Archbishop of Canterbury 139
Toleration Bill ... 139
Tours, Council of ... 53
Tractarian movement 140, 159, 189
Trench, Archbishop of Dublin ... 195
Trent, Council of ... 107
Trinity Sunday, Festival ... 53

U.

Uniformity, Act of ... 106
Urban, Pope ... 40

V.

Vergilius, Archbishop of Arles ... 15
Victoria, Queen ... 143
Vitalian, Pope ... 21

W.

Wales, Church of, Union with English Church ... 48
Waltham, residence of Henry VIII. ... 89
Warham, Archbishop of Canterbury ... 76–88
Wellington, Duke of ... 142, 155
Wesley, John ... 140, 156
Westminster, Council of ... 54
Whitby, Council of ... 24
Whit house, Bishop of Illinois ... 179
Whitgift, Archbishop of Canterbury ... 113
Wighard elected Archbishop of Canterbury ... 21
Wilfrid, Bishop of York ... 24, 31
William of Orange ... 136
William the Conqueror ... 36
William IV. ... 143
Williams, Bishop of Lincoln ... 121
Williams, Dr. Rowland ... 165, 190
Wilson, Rev. H. B. ... 165, 190
Wolsey, Archbishop of York 77, 83
Wordsworth, Bishop of Lincoln ... 170
Wren, Sir Christopher ... 129
Wycliffe, John ... 64
Wykeham, William of ... 141

Y.

York, Duke of ... 130

Z.

Zwinglians ... 79, 103

PRINTED BY WILLIAM CLOWES AND SONS, LIMITED,
LONDON AND BECCLES.

PUBLICATIONS

OF THE

Society for Promoting Christian Knowledge.

THE FATHERS FOR ENGLISH READERS.

A Series of Monograms on the Chief Fathers of the Church, the Fathers selected being centres of influence at important periods of Church History, and in important spheres of action.

Fcap. 8vo, cloth boards, 2s. each.

Leo the Great.
By the Rev. CHARLES GORE, M.A.

Gregory the Great.
By the Rev. J. BARMBY, B.D.

Saint Ambrose: his Life, Times, and Teaching.
By the Rev. ROBINSON THORNTON, D.D.

Saint Athanasius: his Life and Times.
By the Rev. R. WHELER BUSH. (2s. 6d.)

Saint Augustine.
By the Rev. E. L. CUTTS, D.D.

Saint Basil the Great.
By the Rev. RICHARD T. SMITH, B.D.

Saint Bernard, Abbot of Clairvaux, A.D. 1091—1153.
By the Rev. S. J. EALES, M.A., D.C.L. (2s. 6d.)

Saint Hilary of Poitiers, and Saint Martin of Tours.
By the Rev. J. GIBSON CAZENOVE, D.D.

Saint Jerome.
By the Rev. EDWARD L. CUTTS, D.D.

Saint John of Damascus.
By the Rev. J. H. LUPTON, M.A.

Saint Patrick: his Life and Teaching.
By the Rev. E. J. NEWELL, M.A. (2s. 6d.)

Synesius of Cyrene, Philosopher and Bishop.
By ALICE GARDNER.

The Apostolic Fathers.
By the Rev. H. S. HOLLAND.

The Defenders of the Faith; or, The Christian Apologists of the Second and Third Centuries.
By the Rev. F. WATSON, M.A.

The Venerable Bede.
By the Rev. G. F. BROWNE.

THE ROMANCE OF SCIENCE.

A Series of Books which shows that Science has for the masses as great interest as, and more edification than, the romances of the day.

Small Post 8vo, cloth boards.

COAL: and what we get from it.
By Professor RAPHAEL MELDOLA, F.R.S., F.I.C. With numerous illustrations. 2s. 6d.

COLOUR, MEASUREMENT, AND MIXTURE.
By Captain W DE W. ABNEY, C.B., R.E., F.R.S. With several illustrations. 2s. 6d.

THE MAKING OF FLOWERS.
By the Rev. Professor GEORGE HENSLOW, M.A., F.L.S., F.G.S. With several illustrations. 2s. 6d.

DISEASES OF PLANTS.
By H. MARSHALL WARD, M.A., F.R.S., F.L.S. With numerous illustrations. 2s. 6d.

TIME AND TIDE: a Romance of the Moon.
By Sir ROBERT S. BALL, F.R.S., Royal Astronomer of Ireland. Second Edition Revised. Illustrated. 2s. 6d.

THE STORY OF A TINDER-BOX.
By the late CHARLES MEYMOTT TIDY, M.B.M.S., F.C.S. With numerous illustrations. 2s.

THE BIRTH AND GROWTH OF WORLDS.
A Lecture by Professor GREEN, M.A., F.R.S. 1s.

SOAP-BUBBLES, and the Forces which mould them.
By C. V. BOYS, A.R.S.M., F.R.S. With numerous diagrams. 2s. 6d.

SPINNING-TOPS.
By Prof. J. PERRY, M.E., D.Sc., F.R.S. With numerous diagrams. 2s. 6d.

NON-CHRISTIAN RELIGIOUS SYSTEMS.

A Series of Manuals which furnish in a brief and popular form an accurate account of the great Non-Christian Religious Systems of the World.

Fcap. 8vo, cloth boards, 2s. 6d. each.

BUDDHISM: Being a Sketch of the Life and Teachings of Gautama, the Buddha.
By T. W. RHYS DAVIDS. With Map.

BUDDHISM IN CHINA.
By the Rev. S. BEAL. With Map.

CHRISTIANITY AND BUDDHISM: A Comparison and a Contrast.
By the Rev. T. STERLING BERRY, D.D.

CONFUCIANISM AND TAOUISM.
By Professor R. K. DOUGLAS, of the British Museum. With Map.

HINDUISM.
By Sir MONIER WILLIAMS. With Map.

ISLAM AND ITS FOUNDER.
By J. W. H. STOBART. With Map.

ISLAM, as a Missionary Religion.
By CHARLES R. HAINES. (2s.)

THE CORAN: Its Composition and Teaching, and the Testimony it bears to the Holy Scriptures.
By Sir WILLIAM MUIR, K.C.S.I.

DIOCESAN HISTORIES.

This Series furnishes a perfect Library of English Ecclesiastical History. Each volume is complete in itself, and the possibility of repetition has been carefully guarded against.

Fcap. 8vo, cloth boards.

Bath and Wells.
By the Rev. W. HUNT. With Map, 2s. 6d.
Canterbury.
By the Rev. R. C. JENKINS, Hon. Canon of Canterbury. With Map, 3s. 6d.
Carlisle.
By RICHARD S. FERGUSON, Esq. With Map, 2s. 6d.
Chichester.
By the Rev. W. R. W. STEPHENS. With Map and Plan, 2s. 6d.
Durham.
By the Rev. J. L. LOW. With Map and Plan, 2s. 6d.
Hereford.
By the Rev. Canon PHILLOTT. With Map, 3s.
Lichfield.
By the Rev. W. BERESFORD. With Map, 2s. 6d.
Norwich.
By the Rev. A. JESSOPP, D.D. With Map, 2s. 6d.
Oxford.
By the Rev. E. MARSHALL. With Map, 2s. 6d.
Peterborough.
By the Rev. G. A. POOLE, M.A. With Map, 2s. 6d.
Salisbury.
By the Rev. W. H. JONES. With Map and Plan, 2s. 6d.
St. Asaph.
By the Ven. Archdeacon THOMAS. With Map, 2s.
St. David's.
By the Rev. Canon BEVAN. With Map, 2s. 6d.
Winchester.
By the Rev. W. BENHAM, B.D. With Map, 3s.
Worcester.
By the Rev. I. GREGORY SMITH, M.A., and the Rev. PHIPPS ONSLOW, M.A. With Map, 3s. 6d.
York.
By the Rev. Canon ORNSBY, M.A., F.S.A. With Map, 3s. 6d.

CHIEF ANCIENT PHILOSOPHIES.

This Series of Books deals with the chief systems of Ancient Thought, not merely as dry matters of History, but as having a bearing on Modern Speculation.

Fcap. 8vo, cloth boards, 2s. 6d. each.

Aristotelianism.
The Ethics of Aristotle, by the Rev. I. GREGORY SMITH, M.A., Hon. LL.D. The Logical Treatise, the Metaphysics, the Psychology, the Politics, by the Rev. W. GRUNDY, M.A.
Epicureanism.
By W. WALLACE, Esq., Fellow and Tutor of Merton College, Oxford.
Stoicism.
By the Rev. W. W. CAPES, Fellow of Hertford College.

CHURCH HYMNS.

Nos. 1 to 7, in Various Sizes and Bindings, ranging in price from 1d. to 4s. 8d.

CHURCH HYMNS, with Tunes.
Edited by Sir ARTHUR SULLIVAN. Crown 8vo, Fcap. 4to, and Folio (Organ copy), in various Bindings, from 2s. to £1 1s.

COMMON PRAYER-BOOK AND CHURCH HYMNS.
Bound in one Volume, and in Two Volumes in Cases. Can be had in various Sizes and Bindings, from 5d. to 4s.

COMMON PRAYER-BOOK AND CHURCH HYMNS, with Tunes.
Brevier, 8vo, limp paste grain roan, red edges, 6s.

COMMENTARY ON THE BIBLE.

By various Authors. With Maps and Plans.

Crown 8vo, cloth boards, red edges, 4s.; half calf, 10s.; whole calf, 12s.; half morocco, 12s. each volume.

OLD TESTAMENT.
Vol. I., containing the Pentateuch.

OLD TESTAMENT.
Vol. II., containing the Historical Books, Joshua to Esther.

OLD TESTAMENT.
Vol. III., containing the Poetical Books, Job to Song of Solomon.

OLD TESTAMENT.
Vol. IV., containing the Prophetical Books, Isaiah to Malachi.

OLD TESTAMENT.
Vol. V., containing the Apocryphal Books.

NEW TESTAMENT.
Vol. I., containing the Four Gospels.

NEW TESTAMENT.
Vol. II., containing the Acts, Epistles, and Revelation.

ANCIENT HISTORY FROM THE MONUMENTS.

This Series is chiefly intended to illustrate the Sacred Scriptures by the results of recent Monumental Researches in the East. The Volumes have, however, an independent value, as furnishing, as far as they go, thoroughly trustworthy histories of the ancient Monarchies of the Eastern World.

Fcap. 8vo, cloth boards, 2s. each.

ASSYRIA, from the Earliest Times to the Fall of Nineveh.
By the late GEORGE SMITH, of the Department of Oriental Antiquities, British Museum.

BABYLONIA, the History of.
By the late GEORGE SMITH. Edited by the Rev. H. A. SAYCE, Assistant Professor of Comparative Philology, Oxford.

EGYPT, from the Earliest Times to B.C. 300.
By the late S. BIRCH, LL.D.

PERSIA, from the Earliest Period to the Arab Conquest.
By the late W. S. W. VAUX, M.A., F.R.S.

SINAI, from the Fourth Egyptian Dynasty to the Present Time.
By the late H. SPENCER PALMER, Major R.E., F.R.A.S. A new edition, revised throughout by the Rev. Professor SAYCE.

MISCELLANEOUS PUBLICATIONS.

	s.	d.
AIDS TO PRAYER. By the Rev. DANIEL MOORE. Printed in red and black. Post 8vo..........Cloth boards	1	6
ALONE WITH GOD; or, Helps to Thought and Prayer, for the use of the Sick; based on Short Passages of Scripture. By the Rev. F. BOURDILLON, M.A. 12mo..........Cloth boards	1	0
APOSTLE OF THE GENTILES (THE): his Life and Letters. By the Rev. C. R. BALL, M.A. Post 8vo..........Cloth boards	2	6
AUTHENTICITY OF THE GOSPEL OF ST. LUKE (THE): Its Bearing upon the Evidences of the Truth of Christianity. Five Lectures, by the BISHOP OF BATH AND WELLS. Small Post 8vo..........Cloth boards	1	6
BEDSIDE READINGS. By the Rev. F. BOURDILLON, M.A. 12mo..........Cloth boards	2	0
BEING OF GOD, Six Addresses on the. By C. J. ELLICOTT, D.D., Bishop of Gloucester and Bristol. Small Post 8vo..........Cloth boards	1	6
BIBLE PLACES; or, The Topography of the Holy Land. By the Rev. Canon TRISTRAM. With Map and numerous Woodcuts. Crown 8vo..........Cloth boards	4	0
CALLED TO BE SAINTS. The Minor Festivals Devotionally Studied. By CHRISTINA G. ROSSETTI, author of "Seek and Find." Post 8vo. Cloth boards	5	0
CASE FOR "ESTABLISHMENT" STATED (THE). By the Rev. T. MOORE, M.A. Post 8vo..........Paper boards	0	6
CHRISTIANS UNDER THE CRESCENT IN ASIA. By the Rev. E. L. CUTTS, D.D. With numerous Illustrations. Crown 8vo..........Cloth boards	5	0
CHRISTUS COMPROBATOR; or, The Testimony of Christ to the Old Testament. Seven Addresses by C. J. ELLICOTT, D.D., Bishop of Gloucester and Bristol. Small Post 8vo..........Cloth boards	2	0
CHURCH IN THE NEW TESTAMENT, Notes of Lessons on the. By the Rev. E. L. CUTTS, D.D., author of "Turning-Points of Church History," &c. With Map. Crown 8vo. Cloth boards	2	6

PUBLICATIONS OF THE SOCIETY

DEVOTIONAL (A) LIFE OF OUR LORD.   *s. d.*
By the Rev. EDWARD L. CUTTS, D.D., author of "Pastoral Counsels," &c. Post 8vo..............................*Cloth boards*   5   0

DISPENSATION OF THE SPIRIT (THE).
Being Readings on the Person and Work of the Holy Ghost in Relation to the World, the Church, and the Individual. By the Rev. C. R. BALL, M.A. Small Post 8vo. *Cloth boards*   2   6

DIVINE SOCIETY (THE); or, The Church's Care of Large Populations.
Cambridge Lectures on Pastoral Theology, 1890. By the Rev. Canon JACOB. Small Post 8vo.......................*Cloth boards*   2   6

GOSPELS, THE FOUR.
Arranged in the Form of an English Harmony, from the Text of the Authorised Version. By the Rev. J. M. FULLER, M.A. With Analytical Table of Contents and Four Maps. *Cloth boards*   1   0

LAND OF ISRAEL (THE).
A Journal of Travel in Palestine, undertaken with special reference to its Physical Character. By the Rev. Canon TRISTRAM. With two Maps and Illustrations. Large Post 8vo.
Cloth boards   10   6

LECTURES ON THE HISTORICAL AND DOGMATICAL POSITION OF THE CHURCH OF ENGLAND.
By the Rev. W. BAKER, D.D. Post 8vo............*Cloth boards*   1   6

LESSER LIGHTS.
By the Rev. F. BOURDILLON, M.A. SERIES I and II. Post 8vo.
Cloth boards, each   2   6

LETTER AND SPIRIT.
Notes on the Commandments. By CHRISTINA G. ROSSETTI. Post 8vo...*Cloth boards*   2   0

MANUAL OF PAROCHIAL WORK (A).
For the Use of the Younger Clergy. By various Writers. Edited by the Rev. Canon ELLERTON. Large Post 8vo....*Cloth boards*   6   0

MARTYRS AND SAINTS OF THE FIRST TWELVE CENTURIES. Studies from the Lives of the Black-Letter Saints of the English Calendar.
By Mrs. RUNDLE CHARLES. Crown 8vo...........*Cloth boards*   5   0

OURSELVES, OUR PEOPLE, OUR WORK.
Six Addresses given in the Divinity Schools, Cambridge, by the Rev. E. T. LEEKE, M.A. Small Post 8vo.......*Cloth boards*   2   0

PALEY'S EVIDENCES.
A New Edition, with Notes, Appendix, and Preface. By the Rev. E. A. LITTON. Post 8vo........................*Cloth boards*   4   0

PALEY'S HORÆ PAULINÆ.
A New Edition, with Notes, Appendix, and Preface. By the Rev. J. S. Howson, D.D., Dean of Chester. Post 8vo. .... *Cloth boards* **3 0**

PARISH PRIEST OF THE TOWN.
Lectures delivered in the Divinity School, Cambridge, by the Right Rev. J. Gott, D.D. Post 8vo. .... *Cloth boards* **3 0**

PASTORAL COUNSELS; or, Words of Encouragement and Guidance to Holy Living.
By the Rev. E. L. Cutts. Crown 8vo. .... *Cloth boards* **1 6**

PASTORAL THEOLOGY (LECTURES ON), with Special Reference to the Promises required of Candidates for Ordination.
By the late Venerable J. R. Norris, B.D., Archdeacon of Bristol. Post 8vo. .... *Cloth boards* **2 0**

PEACE WITH GOD.
A Manual for the Sick. By the Rev. E. Burbidge, M.A. Post 8vo. .... *Cloth boards* **1 6**

PLAIN WORDS FOR CHRIST.
Being a Series of Readings for Working Men. By the late Rev. R. G. Dutton. Post 8vo. .... *Cloth boards* **1 0**

PRAYER OF CHRISTENDOM, THE GREAT.
By Mrs. Rundle Charles, author of "The Schönberg-Cotta Family." Post 8vo. .... *Cloth boards* **1 6**

PROMISED SEED (THE).
Being a Course of Lessons on the Old Testament, for Schools and Families, arranged for every Sunday in the Year. By the Rev. C. R. Ball, M.A. Post 8vo. .... *Cloth boards* **1 6**

RELIGION FOR EVERY DAY.
Lectures for Men. By the Right Rev. A. Barry, D.D. Fcap. 8vo. .... *Cloth boards* **1 0**

SCENES IN THE EAST.
Consisting of Twelve Coloured Photographic Views of Places mentioned in the Bible, beautifully executed, with Descriptive Letterpress. By the Rev. Canon Tristram.
Cloth, bevelled boards, red edges **6 0**

SEEK AND FIND.
A Double Series of Short Studies of the Benedicite. By Christina G. Rossetti. Post 8vo. .... *Cloth boards* **2 6**

SERVANTS OF SCRIPTURE (THE).
By the late Rev. J. W. Burgon, B.D. Post 8vo. *Cloth boards* **1 6**

SINAI AND JERUSALEM; or, Scenes from Bible Lands. *s. d.*
Consisting of Coloured Photographic Views of Places mentioned in the Bible, including a Panoramic View of Jerusalem, with Descriptive Letterpress. By the Rev. F. W. HOLLAND, M.A., Demy 4to............................*Cloth, bevelled boards, gilt edges* 6 0

SOME CHIEF TRUTHS OF RELIGION.
By the Rev. E. L. CUTTS, D.D., author of "St. Cedd's Cross." Crown 8vo...*Cloth boards* 2 6

THOUGHTS FOR MEN AND WOMEN.
THE LORD'S PRAYER. By EMILY C. ORR. Post 8vo.
Limp cloth 1 0

THOUGHTS FOR WORKING DAYS.
Original and Selected. By EMILY C. ORR. Post 8vo.
Limp cloth 1 0

THREE MARTYRS OF THE NINETEENTH CENTURY: Studies from the Lives of Livingstone, Gordon, and Patteson.
By Mrs. RUNDLE CHARLES. Crown 8vo............*Cloth boards* 3 6

TIME FLIES; a Reading Diary.
By CHRISTINA G. ROSSETTI. Post 8vo.............*Cloth boards* 2 6

TRUE VINE (THE).
By Mrs. RUNDLE CHARLES, author of "The Schönberg-Cotta Family," &c. Printed in red and black. Post 8vo. *Cloth boards* 1 6

TURNING-POINTS OF ENGLISH CHURCH HISTORY.
By the Rev. E. L. CUTTS, D.D., Vicar of Holy Trinity, Haverstock Hill. Crown 8vo................................*Cloth boards* 3 6

TURNING-POINTS OF GENERAL CHURCH HISTORY.
By the Rev. E. L. CUTTS, D.D., author of "Pastoral Counsels." Crown 8vo...*Cloth boards* 5 0

WITHIN THE VEIL.
Studies in the Epistle to the Hebrews. By Mrs. RUNDLE CHARLES, author of "Chronicles of the Schönberg-Cotta Family." Small Post 8vo................................*Cloth boards* 1 6

www.ingramcontent.com/pod-product-compliance
Lightning Source LLC
Chambersburg PA
CBHW031745230426
43669CB00007B/483